Andrei Ostalski

English Rules

A Russo-British Comedy of Errors

Translated from Russian by Alexander Tulloch

English Rules. A Russo-British Comedy of Errors. By Andrei Ostalski
©Andrei Ostalski 2013

All rights reserved by the author

ISBN: 978-1-291-55763-3

PublishNation London
www.publishnation.co.uk

CHAPTER ONE

The clown strikes

The train was due in three minutes. Sashok was already craning his neck impatiently, trying to catch sight of the first carriage, waiting for it to poke its flat face out from behind the white cliffs of Dover when, from behind, a set of iron fingers grabbed hold of his right wrist. The pain lasted just for a second – Sashok emitted a quiet yelp – and then subsided. His hand was free again but the black, imitation leather briefcase that his father-in-law had given him for his birthday just a month earlier, was gone. Sashok turned around, and what he saw nearly made him cry out a second time. He had seen all sorts on the platforms of Folkestone Central: Kosovars, Arabs, Chinese, but this... this was unheard of. Grinning from ear to ear was a man wearing a quilted jacket and a Russian peasant's cap with ear-flaps. And his feet: his feet were immersed in a pair of valenki – the traditional felt boots of Russian peasants. He was dressed like a clown, like a clumsy parody of a Russian, and looked as if he had just walked off the latest Doctor Zhivago or James Bond film set. 'He's wearing felt boots....with galoshes!' Sashok couldn't believe his eyes. But he didn't have enough time to marvel at the galoshes because he suddenly remembered the briefcase. And here was the problem – and quite an incredible problem at that: the briefcase had cloned itself. Huddled together, cheek by jowl, there on the platform were two black briefcases, indistinguishable, like identical twins.

'Don't just stand there, pick one, any one. Whichever one you like!' the man in the felt boots said in Russian, smirking unpleasantly.

And Sashok was indeed just standing there, unable to utter a word. He was about to open his mouth and speak. 'What do you think you're doing?' he wanted to ask, but decided against it at the last minute. Somehow he couldn't bring himself to talk to this clown in English. And the only Russian that came to mind was – quite unexpectedly – an obscenity. Sashok suppressed it, because he never swore.

Strangely enough, no one on the platform seemed to be paying them the slightest attention. Neither the clown in his ridiculous outfit, nor the two identical briefcases at his feet seemed to provoke the slightest interest in the dutiful commuters, growing impatient as they waited for their train, waiting, as they did day after day, to cram themselves into their British trains and be whisked off to work in another town.

'Well, suit yourself. If you won't pick one, I will. I haven't got time for a staring competition,' the man in the felt boots announced. He briefly ran a stubby finger with its black fingernail over first one briefcase and then the other, muttering, 'Eniki-Byeniki-yeli-varyeniki....' And then in heavily accented English, 'Eenie meenie minie mo, catch a piggie by its toe....' Here he paused. Then, with a decisive 'Aha!' he grabbed the briefcase nearest to him, turned on his heels and set off towards the exit, engulfed by the flow of oncoming human traffic.

'Wait!' Sashok squeaked, 'this isn't on....' He was about to run after the buffoon, but would he have caught him? Could he have fought his way through the deluge of commuters moving inexorably towards him? In any case, the 7:07 to Charing Cross had in the meantime already materialised on platform 1, announcing itself by the thunder of its steel doors as they slammed against the sides of the vintage carriages, built no doubt some time in the fifties or sixties, or even before the war. And now the guard's shrill, menacing whistle, the train's about to pull out, and if he missed it he would have to stand out in the sun for another half hour till the next one arrived. Then he'd be late for work and his boss, Mr Singh, would put him in the dog-house again, and Sashok would have to endure a day of contemptuous sideways glances. So, having weighed up the options, he cast his eye over the remaining briefcase, ran his hands over all four corners ('seems to be mine, thank God!') and at the very last minute hurled himself onto the train, followed by a barrage of reproachful bawling and whistling from the guard.

He settled himself into a seat by the window furthest away from the aisle. Now perhaps he would be able to travel all the way to London in relative comfort, since the British, for some reason (here's the national character for you) cannot bear to sit in the middle, hemmed in on both sides, and actually, on occasions, prefer to stand. Consequently, where there were three seats together, as opposed to just two, the lucky ones could sit back and relax. The superiority of three-seaters over two-seaters, in fact, was the one advantage of travelling 'cattle-class', but nevertheless one that could make life a little more bearable. But here again, the rule did not always hold true. For when push came to shove – and that it did every single day during the evening rush-hour – the tired commuter would cram himself into his train carriage like a herring in a barrel. And now we can forget the subtleties of English individualism: sitting or standing, quiet as lambs, the passengers take up every square inch of available space.

In fact, Sashok had many questions on the subject of English trains. The problem was who to ask? He could turn to his wife, Anna-Maria, but her reactions were unpredictable: she might purse her lips as if she suspected him of 'point scoring'. This is how it had been the last time, when he had made a slightly barbed comment about rhubarb tea. As for his father-in-law John (he still couldn't get used to calling him by his first name), and his mother-in-law Maggie it was better to steer clear of such topics with them. There would be the inevitable sighs, the exchange of meaningful glances and expressions of disappointment on their faces. Not that they were conceited fools, far from it. On occasion, they could even manage some light self-deprecatory humour. But whenever Sashok opened his mouth they took everything the wrong way, with that look of how-could-you-be-so-tactless, as if he had some kind of hidden agenda. What is it the English say about the pot calling the kettle black?

And so his list of questions just got longer and longer. Why, for example, were the trains always late? It would be one thing if they were, let's say, sometimes or even often late. But with such precise regularity? And why the hell that ancient rolling stock, those museum piece carriages with twenty doors each (ten on either side)? At first Sashok had assumed that they were there to amuse the tourists, a little bit of exotica like the black cabs and red phone booths, post boxes and so on. But then, reading the Evening Standard, he realised, that the commuters themselves hated their trains and journalists were ashamed of them. 'You'd have to search pretty hard to find such trains in the third world' wailed the embarrassed author of one article. It was from this same article that he had gleaned the expression "cattle-class". Apart from all the various guises of second class, there was of course first class. And here was a horror all of its own. Sashok had once been privileged to sample its charms, when the conductor allowed everybody to grab a seat anywhere they could because half the carriages had been taken out of service due to the fact that they were 'not in working order'. The dustiness, stuffiness and darkness of those disgusting compartments completely stumped him. Why pay significant sums of money for such torture? He had two working hypotheses: either it was yet another manifestation of the famous English stoicism, an utterly superfluous test of the stiffness of the stiff upper lip. The only other solution had to be that the unions and the Labour Party were conspiring with other assorted leftists to punish the rich.

And he had another question: why do young and even some middle-aged Englishmen put their dirty feet on the seats opposite? And not just hippie-types either; quite respectable-looking men and women are sometimes as guilty. And the ticket collector (who doubles as a sort of attendant or conductor but is generally referred to in English as 'the guard' –is he there to protect us?) comes along and checks our tickets and sometimes punches holes in them with steel clippers with such force that little round bits of cardboard fly off in all directions (one of these bits hit Sashok in the eye one day). And why, finally, in the toilets.... Sh-sh, no, better not speak of the toilets, after all we're talking about a state which is a permanent member of the U.N. Security Council.

Sashok was awakened from his musings by the sudden recollection of his as yet unchecked article for the journal 'Investment in the Former Soviet Union'. He leapt to his feet as if he had been stung and reached for his briefcase. 'I hope I haven't left it at home, or that'll be it, curtains, sacked by the merciless Indian,' he thought, as he tried feverishly to unlock the case. But whether it was because he was fumbling, or for some other reason, he couldn't get the damned thing to open. It struck him that the lock might have jammed. This had happened before, but a little gentle insistence, a pull here, a tug there, was usually sufficient for it to give in. But no, this time it was well and truly stuck. Sashok looked around the carriage: the man diagonally opposite was buried deep in his copy of The Times, paying him not the slightest attention. But the nasty-looking old woman on the right across the aisle was showing clear signs of interest. Oh, to hell with you, Sashok thought, look on, enjoy the show, but blushed all the same: what was going through her mind? He gave the leather strap a decisive yank to the right: no luck. He jerked it to the left: nothing. He gathered all his strength and pressed down on the round lock. Useless! As he tugged, squeezed and pushed, trying to ignore the old lady to his right, getting hotter and hotter under the collar and hoping for the lock to break or the belt to snap, he imagined having to explain himself to his father-in-law....

'Where the hell's the key? I haven't got it. It must be in my wife's desk,' he thought.

Then suddenly his concentration snapped and he remembered the idiotic episode on the platform with the idiotic Russian clown.... So the old woman had been right all along: the briefcase Sashok was so busy mauling was not his own, which was of course why it wouldn't open!

'He switched them after all, the damned joker, he got away with his filthy little prank!' Sashok thought.

By now the man opposite had surfaced from behind his newspaper and was staring fixedly at him. Sashok froze, clutching the ill-fated briefcase to his knees with both hands.

'Of course it's not mine! I don't remember that scratch. And mine was heavier. Why didn't I notice it straight away?'

And then it came to him, clear as daylight. It was obvious. It was not a prank after all but something much more sinister. Surely, there was a more logical explanation. Like in the movies. But this doesn't happen to inoffensive Russian intellectuals from provincial English town, does it?

Looking at it objectively however, then really it was clear that his fellow-countryman on the platform had just been acting the fool, when what he actually wanted was to use him, Sashok, for his own nefarious ends. And the plan had clearly been a resounding success. But what are they using me for? Sashok wondered, relentlessly following his own line of reasoning. And, just as relentlessly, the answer presented itself: as a cou-ri-er!

'Just keep calm, don't faint', Sashok told himself. 'Sit down and think about it.'

Then he asked himself what could be in this locked briefcase which belonged to somebody else. The first and most obviously cinematic possibility: drugs. Sashok had a vivid image of little bags stuffed with what looked like ground chalk. The second option was money: a million pounds Sterling in pink fifties, each sporting a beautiful representation of Her Majesty. This somehow seemed a less frightening prospect. And finally, theory number three: some kind of top secret documents, whose contents could compromise someone unimaginably omnipotent, like the boss of some big Siberian oil company, the director of the FSB, or at least the CIA. Sashok concluded that apart from the obvious three, there was in fact a multitude of other possibilities, none of which promised glamorous adventure, but which were rather fraught with danger to life and limb, not to mention reputation. Somewhere deep inside his soul he still harboured the flickering hope that the whole thing would turn out to be some silly gag, some sick prank, some strange practical joke intended as a reminder of home. But the key thing was to decide what to do next. Go to the police? That would really be a little precipitate. The first thing was to establish beyond reasonable doubt that the briefcase had actually been switched. Otherwise he'd look like the biggest fool on earth. 'Either way, I've got to get this case open', Sashok decided. 'I've got to open it no matter what.'

CHAPTER TWO

The madman's briefcase

On the sixth floor of Century Building (on the corner of Montrose Road and Mill Hill Lane), sitting on a toilet seat in a cubicle in the women's lavatories we see a young man, misery etched into his Russian features. He is attempting to prise open a large briefcase (made of imitation leather) using a pair of outsized office scissors. The scissors are not the ideal tool for the job, and the young man is showing clear signs of agitation, his brow bathed in sweat, his hands trembling from the exertion, his eyes bulging in their sockets. But his current monstrous appearance is deceptive – when he is more relaxed he's really not that bad looking: large brown eyes, regular facial features and slightly curly blond hair. Perhaps he's a little on the lean side, or 'rather skinny' as his wife Anna Maria would say, which would translate into Russian as 'skin and bones'. 'It's what's inside that counts,' she probably whispers, when she thinks Sashok can't hear her.

The day had started badly. First of all he had overstayed his allocated time in the bathroom by a whole five minutes, thereby putting the entire family timetable out of kilter. As a result, he'd had to run to the station, where he had been accosted by some guy with an identical briefcase to his own. And that was not the end of his troubles: on top of everything else, the train had sat outside London Bridge station for twenty minutes. When he finally got off the train, Sashok sped across the bridge like a wild boar, paying close attention to his breathing, anticipating the movement of the crowd and scurrying through the gaps almost without incident. At one point he swerved out really rather nimbly into the road, only to slip back into the human flow moments later. Pity they don't make this commuter's slalom an Olympic sport, he thought, I would probably qualify for a medal. But despite his efforts, he was fifteen minutes late for work. Inevitably, he failed to slip in unnoticed, and Mr Singh (Sashok got his revenge for everything by calling him Sinyukha) emerged ceremoniously from his accursed little cubby-hole to greet him, ostentatiously examining his watch. "Good morning, sir", he said in a distinctly unfriendly tone and in full hearing of the entire office. 'Good morning, Mr Singh, how are you? I am so sorry. Excuse me. The train....' Sashok mumbled.

'You do remember that today is Friday? And that means the deadline for the entire journal. Where is the article on Moldovan textiles?'

'All I need is another half an hour, sir, just to put in the corrections.'

What really riled him though, was the fact that his article really was almost finished. He had taken a print-out with him the day before, so as to work on it a bit on the train. In the end, he had continued working on the paper at home well into the night, to the annoyance of the whole family. Now, of course, his article was in the briefcase. Or rather, in one of two briefcases: either in the one Sashok had with him in his hand, or in the one pilfered by that joker in the quilted jacket.

After his brief but unpleasant exchange with Mr Singh, Sashok sat down at his desk, placed the briefcase on the floor and looked around him. The excitement caused by his late arrival and his dressing-down from the boss had subsided, and the workforce once again had their noses up against their computer screens. The place next to him, usually occupied by Liz the admin girl, was empty. But there on the desk, in all its glory – yes, this was what he had been pinning his hopes on – sat a tankard emblazoned with a Maltese cross. Poking out enticingly over the rim of the mug was an outsized pair of office scissors. His colleagues appeared to be minding their own business. Go on then! Grab them while no one's watching! Sashok hesitated for a few seconds longer as he attempted to muster all his courage. By the time he finally reached out uncertainly for the scissors it was too late: at that precise moment Vugar, his Azeri colleague, tore his gaze away from his monitor and turned to him, about to say something. Then, as if responding to some unseen signal, Czech Volodimir and Lee, the Russian Korean, followed suit. Even Tsveta, the usually impervious Bulgarian girl, turned around. Sashok froze in an unnatural pose, right arm extended and a sheepish grin on his face.

He had been unlucky like that all his life. He tried cheating twice at school but got caught both times. By the time he got to university he had given up trying, and could only look on with envy as his classmates enthusiastically and vigorously employed this effective grade-enhancing tactic without qualms or adverse consequences. He was always losing money, never finding it. No, that's not quite true. Once, back in the days of the Soviet Union in Moscow, he found a ten rouble note on the street. And what do you think? Immediately he was accosted by some bruiser who grabbed him by the shoulders and shouted, 'Hey, that's mine. I just dropped it.' He then snatched the money out of Sashok's hand and headed straight for the booze shop. In fact, now that he came to think of it, that bloke had borne a striking resemblance to this morning's clown in the felt boots. Might they be related?

The memory of that incident galvanised Sashok back into action. What was it his old class-mate Gavrilov used to say when he got caught? If in doubt, brazen it out. Sashok pulled a face at his meddling colleagues, grabbed the scissors and set off towards the toilets, nearly knocking his chair over on the way. But to get there he had to pass right by Mr Singh's cubicle. Inevitably, his boss got off the phone at exactly that moment and fixed his eyes on Sashok. He smiled and carried on, briefcase in one hand, scissors in the other, as if this was the most natural thing in the world. To hell with him, he thought, to the winner the spoils. I'll get this damned thing open, find my print-out, and get down to business. Put in the corrections, hand in the report, everything will be fine and my little trip to the loo with the briefcase and scissors will be written off as a minor eccentricity. If on the other hand the report isn't there....

No, bad luck is one thing, but this was beyond a joke. Never in his life had he encountered both toilet cubicles occupied at the same time. But there it was, no matter how much he pulled and tugged on the handle, the doors would not budge. Should he push, perhaps? It could be embarrassing and, you never know, he might break the bolt. Strangely, there was no sound whatsoever coming from within the cubicles. Had he scared the occupants?

Just then Lee, the Russian Korean, came in. He looked at Sashok (still with his briefcase in one hand and the scissors in the other) and headed towards the urinals.

'Oh, by the way, the cubicles are closed for repairs,' he announced sadly, facing the wall.

'But what am I supposed to do?' Sashok wailed. His voice must have struck such a tragic note, that Lee craned his head round and said sympathetically,

'You were late, you see. Mr Singh made the announcement early this morning. He said that if anyone was really desperate they could use the ladies.'

'Was he joking?'

'Not at all, he was dead serious.... Don't worry, go on, it's perfectly normal.'

So that's how Sashok found himself in the women's toilets on the sixth floor of Century Building. To hell with my father-in-law he thought, gritting his teeth. I'll open this damned briefcase even if I have to cut it to pieces! Nevertheless, he couldn't help imagining the resulting conversation with his father-in-law, his thin lips puckered in disbelief, while his mother-in-law stared unblinkingly into the far corner. They'll take me for an idiot, and they'd be right, a thousand times right, Sashok grumbled as he desperately attacked the wretched lock with the scissors. And then, just as he was about to give up in despair, the lock began to creak, then started to give way, and finally came off at the hinges. The first thing to fly out of the briefcase was a large tome with a cover that had seen better days. Sashok caught it before it landed on the cubicle floor. This was followed by a new-ish lady's training shoe, left foot. But it was the book that caught Sashok's stupefied eye. It was called.... Well, there were two lines to the title, the first of which read: Diccionario Ecologico Luso – Japones. The second line was gobbledegook. As far as he could tell it was a dictionary of ecological terminology. A dictionary for those who, unlike Sashok, knew a language called Luso, and were interested in Japanese. Or perhaps the other way around.

Right, Sashok said to himself calmly, the main thing is to keep a hold of yourself and think logically. And so, how likely was it that he had left the house with someone else's book by accident? Quite possible. In fact, this had happened before. Once for example, he had picked up his father-in-law's statistical analysis of the month of February and set off to work with it. To this day he had no idea how it had happened. So, on to the next question. The key word was obviously Ecology. His family was ideologically enlightened on environmental issues, and he had been dragged along to various lectures and seminars on more than one occasion. Indeed, were it not for a certain reticence on Sashok's part – and all manner of hastily improvised excuses – he would have been dragged to many more. On the other hand, as far as he knew, nobody in the family had a clue about Japanese or (what was it?) Luso. And what about the trainer? Sashok thrust his hand deeper into the briefcase and pulled out: a magnifying glass with a black plastic handle that had clearly been broken once upon a time and had now been stuck on with scotch tape, a CD case (empty) entitled "Songs of Ancient Tuva", two copies of the Russian weekly Argumenty I Fakty, health supplement dated last year and a yellowing copy of The Morning Star. The next handful produced an outsized alarm clock that had clearly stopped a long time ago and was beginning to rust and a pack of cards, or rather half the deck, just the black cards, the clubs and spades. His article was nowhere to be found, and nor were his own newspapers and magazines. There was no sign either of Roman Gary's 'Promise at Dawn" or his Chinese-made calculator, his note-book or his beloved filofax. For all his absent-mindedness, surely he could not possibly have forgotten all his own things on this occasion and mechanically collected all this junk instead! Sashok's long-held suspicion now became an absolute certainty: the briefcase belonged to someone else. He tried not to panic and to work out the ramifications of his discovery. First of all, the article on Moldova would have to be done from scratch. He would now have to demonstrate wonderful powers of concentration, efficiency and inspiration if he was to hand it in on time. It hardly seemed realistic to hope that the blighter in the quilted jacket would pop up like a Jack-in-a-box exclaiming, 'Ha-ha, I really got you, didn't I?!' and return his briefcase together with the article. Further, it was clear that the switch had been some kind of prank, albeit a strange, not to say insane one. But he was comforted by the fact that nobody had planted explosives, drugs or counterfeit money on him. All in all, Sashok concluded, it could have been worse.

In the meantime, someone had entered the ladies'. Sashok froze, clutching the scissors in one hand and the alarm clock in the other, petrified that any sound might give him away. Whoever it was, and it could have been any one of his colleagues, male or female, sat down in the adjoining cubicle, and Sashok winced as he was forced to listen to all the usual noises. Then there was a long period of hand-washing, followed by an equally lengthy drying process. Then he heard Tsveta's voice, 'Sasha, are you there? Are you all right?' Startled, he dropped the clock, which crashed to the floor and embarked on an ear-piercing, deafening ring. It filled the whole toilet, the whole floor; in fact the whole of Century Building reverberated with the noise. That at least is how it seemed to Sashok as he feverishly fiddled with the buttons and levers protruding from the ancient mechanism. But it was no good. The alarm-clock refused to shut up. It just rang and rang, shuddering in Sashok's hands like some angry little beast.

They came running from all directions.

CHAPTER THREE

No arms allowed

It has to be said that the English are an unpredictable bunch. Sashok was sure that the first question his family would ask after an awkward silence would be something along the lines of, 'and how did they manage to extract you from the women's toilets?' And in fact there would have been nothing to tell. They didn't have to extract him. He emerged from the cubicle of his own accord, brandishing a tattered briefcase, an enormous pair of scissors and a rusty old alarm-clock. He had no particular desire to go into the details of how the wretched machine, having previously seemed beyond use, had suddenly sprung to life as it came into contact with the tiled floor of the toilet and had deafened the entire building. Neither did he wish to remind himself of the way his colleagues had looked at him, especially his boss, Mr Singh. His trip to the ladies' (what else could he do, since the gents' was under repair?), scissors and briefcase in hand, in full view of his colleagues, had no doubt set tongues wagging. Had their Russian friend finally lost it? Then there was the sound of the alarm and all the shouting.... OK, so his briefcase was ripped to pieces, and OK, the alarm-clock he was clutching suddenly went off. Happens to the best of us.

Sashok rehearsed his speech all the way home. He knew that it had to be delivered in a relaxed, confident manner. The thing was to set the right tone from the word go; he wanted to prevent them making fun of him and avoid those subtleties of the English which allow them to appear serious on the surface when, underneath, they are gently teasing you. He could just picture John, his father-in-law, inquiring deadpan: 'The alarm clock, did it carry on ringing very long?' (In actual fact – a full two minutes sixteen seconds). He could do without these Anglo-Saxon jibes.

But the jibes never came. Or at least if they did, they were too subtle for Sashok to notice and what you don't understand can't harm you. He took the right tactical approach: on arriving home, instead of trying to slip in unnoticed he strode straight into the living room, into the eye of the storm, as he was, ruined briefcase and all, impervious to the inevitable exclamations: 'What's wrong?' 'What's happened?' 'Were you attacked?' 'We did warn you there are pickpockets at London Bridge!' 'Or was it one of those ghastly seagulls?' To give them their due, they did sound more concerned about Sashok's personal well-being than the fate of his briefcase. And, on the surface at least, there were no expressions of disbelief. Indeed, Sashok himself hardly believed his own story as he recounted how he had fallen victim to a practical joke (as he now realized) on the way to work. He had had his briefcase switched by some ruffian who had befuddled him with a nursery rhyme and then run off. He hadn't twigged at first; he had just thought that the lock was jammed and he needed to get it open quickly to sort things out. And then came the most difficult part.

'Honestly, John,' said Sashok 'I'm really sorry, but there was nothing else I could do; I had to force the lock off completely. And the article on Moldovan textiles.....today was the deadline. If I hadn't handed it in on time I would have been in real trouble and Mr Singh might even have sacked me.'

At first, Sashok tried not to look them in the eye. He was afraid that the look of disbelief in their eyes would make him lose his nerve; he would inevitably blush and look even more of a fool than he already did. But he finished his monologue and looked up cautiously. Staring back at him were three faces: his father-in-law, serious; his mother-in-law upset; and his wife Anna-Maria wide-eyed and worried. For some reason they dispensed with the awkward probing questions designed to catch him out. Say what you like about the English, they know how to dissemble! Finally, John cleared his throat and... 'But the article, the article on Moldovan textiles, did you hand it in on time?'

Oh, what an inspired question! And one to which there was a splendid answer.

'Of course!' Sashok said in a clear voice, loudly and proudly. 'Of course. I skipped lunch, nose to the grindstone, worked like a galley slave and did it all again from scratch.'

'Oh, that's all that matters, really!' exclaimed his mother-in-law Maggie.

'Yes, that's the main thing! Well done Sasha!' chimed in father-in-law and wife, the yea-sayers, the wretches.

They always took their line from Maggie. Sashok decided to take a little of the wind out of their sails.

'They still didn't get the journal in on time, though. But not because of me,' he said.

'Oh but that's a different matter entirely – an entirely different matter,' his English relatives pronounced, almost in unison.

Sashok was touched. Maybe they're not so dreadful after all. But here he checked himself abruptly. This is no time to get sentimental. Remember the dressing-down they gave you when you put your foot in it over Down's syndrome...A bit incorrect, certainly, but the joke really was funny. And it wasn't at all malicious. I am as sympathetic as the next man about Down's syndrome, but that doesn't mean that one can't make a joke.

Sashok's musings on the mentally-impaired brought back the memory of the joker in the quilted jacket. 'Have a look at what that fool had in his briefcase,' said Sashok as he emptied the contents onto the coffee table. His astonished relatives beheld the following:

A weighty tome entitled Diccionario Luso-Japones;

A magnifying glass, its black handle held together with scotch tape;

Several Russian newspapers, mostly Argumenty i Fakty, health supplement;

A yellowing copy of The Morning Star dated 12th January 1979;

A greasy ball of string;

Half a deck of cards (only the clubs and spades);
Scraps of paper;
A large rusty alarm clock.

His relations crowded around the little coffee table examining each object in turn with keen interest.

'Well, how do you like that?' Sashok exclaimed. 'A primary-school prank!'

'Maybe there's some hidden meaning behind it all?' Anna-Maria suggested.

'Indeed,' echoed Maggie. 'Why just the black cards? There must be some kind of symbolism there... I read something about that once, do you remember, darling? Something dark. And then there's The Morning Star. That's that communist paper, isn't it? And look, it's from '79! Isn't that the year that Gorbachev became a member of the Politburo?' ('How on earth does she know such things?' Sashok gasped. He himself could never remember facts when he read political biographies.)

'Here's a clue if ever I saw one,' Maggie gave her daughter a meaningful look.

Everyone understood what she meant. She was referring to the circumstances under which Sashok met his wife. They had met in 1991, on the barricades in front of the Moscow White House. In truth, Sashok was there purely by accident. He wasn't much of a political animal. But Anna-Maria was fired by the romance of a free Russia. Later of course, she had become disillusioned with Russian capitalism but still got Sashok to marry her and then brought him back home.

'Oh, I shouldn't think so.' Sashok replied. 'We've come a long way since then.' No sooner had he uttered the words, than he regretted them. John's face fell visibly.

'I'm afraid I shall have to leave you. I must look over some papers before bed', he muttered, getting up.

There you go! Sashok had clearly done something wrong, or said something inappropriate. But what? He didn't for the life of him understand. It was always like this. Just when he was thinking what a sound bunch they really were, the kind of people you could have a sensible conversation with, suddenly something would go 'snap!' and the lines of communication would break down. And then he'd have to guess which taboo he'd broken this time, what he'd done to give away his inadequate grasp of convention and those unwritten English rules. And he couldn't always rely on Anna-Maria to come to his rescue. Occasionally she would hint at the nature of the crime committed, but more often than not she would purse her lips, which were quite thin at the best of times, and move the conversation on to a different topic. Maggie followed her husband submissively, though it seemed to Sashok that this time she wasn't keen to go.

She hesitated in the doorway and turned around.

'Have a look, is there a queen of spades in the pack? And what kind of language is that, Luso?'

Neither Sashok nor Anna-Maria could answer the second question, so they quickly dug out the queen of spades. Not that it helped them much.

Alone with his wife at last, Sashok felt a sense of relief. Even Anna-Maria cheered up a little, and they started playing a light-hearted game, trying to guess what this or that object might mean. Should they not, for example, be searching for a numerological code in a Tchaikovsky libretto? And the ball of string: didn't it hint at some kind of reprisal, the threat of physical violence? And the shredded paper – what kind of symbol was that? The alarm-clock of course could well be a hidden reference to how quickly time passes ('That's what we Russians call switching on the meter – you pay for every second', Sashok added.) It goes without saying that all of these remarks were made in that semi-ironic jocular tone the English reserve for all but the most serious of issues. But Sashok had lived in an English family long enough to know that the tone in which something was said did not necessarily mean anything in particular – it could in fact serve as a disguise for one of the many English complexes. He himself even enjoyed playing along with his wife's games from time to time to show that he couldn't be had that easily.

Then Anna-Maria uttered the word that had been on the tip of Sashok's own tongue,

'The police. Why don't we just go to the professionals, instead of playing guessing games ourselves?'

But then, without so much as a pause for breath or a hint of irony, she proceeded to recount stories from the press about how the police were overloaded as it was, with cases of murder, grievous bodily harm and racial discrimination.

'You must have heard, they don't even come out to investigate robberies any more. And they never catch anyone anyway. Remember when they nicked my bag on the Strand last year? No one did anything about it at all. Just think how stupid you'll look. Imagine their line of questioning. 'So you had your briefcase switched? I see... Playing cards and an alarm clock, you say? I-i-interesting! And what charges do you propose to bring? Crime against the person or crime against property?'

'All right, I give in,' said Sashok, 'but we've got to do something!'

Just then Maggie poked her head around the door. She seemed to be dressed for bed.

'I've just popped in to say goodnight. By the way, it's just occurred to me, you know what I'd do if I were you? I'd put an ad in the paper.' With that she cast Sashok what he took to be a reproachful look and retired.

In fact, Sashok understood perfectly well the reasons for the undercurrent of domestic tension. Amongst his acquaintances he'd be hard-pushed to name another couple living in this extended family set-up. In Britain this is not the normal way of doing things. People either rent flats or buy their own homes with a long-term loan secured on the property which is called a mortgage. This, of course, is the right way of going about things. But what could they do? He and Anna-Maria were permanently broke. Her social work paid her peanuts and he just couldn't find a steady job or anything that was remotely well-paid.

'Mother is right; why don't we put an ad in The Guardian?' Anna-Maria's distant voice interrupted his musings.

'Why The Guardian? Why not The Times? Or The Sun for that matter?' replied Sashok.

This upset her. Why, just because the man was poorly dressed did he immediately assume that he was semi-literate and only read right-wing or tabloid papers? She had noticed this snobbish tendency among Russians before. And just because the man wasn't dressed properly...

'You didn't see what he was wearing! Quilted jacket! Felt boots! Galoshes! A hat with ear flaps!'

'So? Why shouldn't a man wear his national dress? Why is it all right for Arabs to walk around in their robes, Indians in their saris, Africans in their multi-coloured whatever they call them, but not for a Russian to wear ear-flaps and a quilted jacket?'

'You really think the quilted jacket is our national costume?' Sashok wailed with a helpless wave of his arm. These English! It was useless trying to explain anything to them. Sashok found them hard to cohabitate with, quite honestly. But then there wasn't much left for him back home in his native Moscow either. He hadn't exactly been living the high life back then, but now, what with the stories he heard from visiting Muscovites about the horrors of life "on the make", the very thought of returning home made him shudder. This was no place for an intellectual past his sell-by date. And, for all her eccentricities, he was really rather fond of Anna-Maria. If only they could somehow jettison her parents... When they were around she became somehow alien, somehow too... too English. That was it! Sashok found it impossible to define quite what this English-ness consisted of. On his rare trips back home, whenever his friends questioned him on the subject, he would say, 'Well, the thing is, my wife writes wonderful poems and lyrics, but if I catch her at it, she'll pretend to be writing a letter to the local council. It's somehow shameful to stand out from the crowd or to aspire to something out of the ordinary. Boasting is completely taboo however much you may want to from time to time. And then, of course, there's the famous English hypocrisy, which isn't even hypocrisy really but a kind of conspiracy of unwritten and unintelligible rules.'

Sashok and Anna-Maria sat there for a long time, looking at each other in silence. He was about to get up and go to bed when his wife suddenly said in a conciliatory tone,

'You know what? Put the ad in that Russian paper, 'Pulse-UK' or 'Angliya.''

Anna-Maria was adamant that Sashok should keep abreast of what was going on in London's Russian community. She would save £1.50 on something or other – Sashok suspected on her lunch though she denied it - to regularly buy him one of these weeklies, and sometimes both. If Anna-Maria had been a Russian wife, Sashok would have kissed her right then and there. And, had she been Russian, she might have cheered up and even kissed him back. But to an Englishwoman, such an open demonstration of emotions was unthinkable. And so Sashok, trying to show off his impeccable grasp of the local customs, replied deadpan,

'Do you really think so?'

And she, being English, nodded confidently without so much as batting an eyelid, meaning: Yes, that is really what I think.

'Well....' Sashok replied dryly by way of agreement, and that settled the matter. They spent the next half hour trying to formulate the wording of the advertisement. For inspiration, they scanned some of the examples in the current issue: 'Philosopher's stones, wholesale and retail' 'Russian lady awaits your call' 'Seeking a veteran of the Great Patriotic War'. Nice, but not quite what they were after.... Anna-Maria was particularly tickled by 'Had enough of the poisonous exhaust fumes of Evil and Moral Decay? Phone....'

'Now this is a bit more like it,' said Sashok, 'If you were using the services of Roman and Vladimir to acquire British papers, please call....' Or 'Anton Malashevsky, get in touch, or else....'

Sashok could already picture poor Anton's creditors, wracked by guilt and crossing themselves, nonetheless managing to carry out the unspecified 'else'.

'What does that mean?' Anna-Maria didn't get it.

'It means, the heavies are after him, killers, that's what it means,' Sashok explained, adding a dash of sang-froid for effect.

'You are kidding!'

'I'm not, but let's hope that the authors of the advert are.'

But assassins and threats in general were not really Sashok's style. He would have to appeal to the man's conscience. Here's what he wrote:

'Fellow-countryman who switched briefcases with me last week at Folkestone-Central station! A joke, if that's what it was, has been appreciated. I suggest switching back urgently. Please call....'

'Well, he's hardly going to accept a briefcase that's been ripped to shreds. Write: 'swap contents of briefcase,' Anna-Maria suggested.

'We'll cross that bridge when we come to it. Let's just hope he calls.'

'Not much hope of that, I'm afraid....' she sighed.

But he did phone, that very same Saturday, as soon as the latest edition of Pulse UK appeared on the newsstands. As luck would have it, Sashok just happened to be passing the phone as it rang, and answered himself. He immediately recognised the voice: sharp, wining and impudent. Not so much as a Good Day or Good Bye, or even a Hello, but straight to the point,

'All right, no problem mate, let's swap'em back. I could be in trouble if I don't get the clock.'

'Let's meet at the station, at Folkestone Central,' suggested the delighted Sashok.

'Not likely. We'll meet at New Cross. You know the station? Seven fifteen in the evening. And make sure you're alone. And unarmed!'

'Un-armed?! But I....' Sashok protested, but he was interrupted.

'Or else....' said the stern voice in the receiver. Then the line went dead.

CHAPTER FOUR

A Narrow-eyed fiend

New Cross, it goes without saying, is no mainline terminus, but a suburban station serving the local community. In fact it is difficult to understand why it was built at all, considering that the more imposing Saint John's, associated as it is with the famous hospital, is just a third of a mile away. The area's principal landmark is Millwall stadium, where the most violent football fans in the whole of Britain, and possibly the world, are said to reign supreme. But it's easier to get there from London by way of another line, which runs via South Bermondsey station.

At peak hour New Cross station is crowded, but, standing on the platform for half an hour, coping with the ebb and flow of the waves of civil servants, Sashok came to the conclusion that the clown was not going to turn up. True, Sashok had no more than a hazy memory of what the strange man looked like, dressed in a quilted jacket, valenki, galoshes, and a hat with ear-flaps, who just a few days earlier had swapped brief-cases with him for some unknown reason. This stupid prank had put Sashok into an unbelievably awkward situation both at work and with his English relatives. His boss and his family members found it difficult to believe his unlikely story (if they believed it at all).

Here, it is true, there was an additional unpleasant nuance: circumstances forced Sashok to rip the whole lock off somebody else's briefcase. Repairing it was out of the question, and Sashok, after talking it over with Anna-Maria, decided not to even take it with him to the rendezvous. God only knew, considering all that had happened, how this nut-case would react when he saw the state of his property. To hell with him, thought Sashok, let him keep the gift he got from his father-in-law, even if it was totally unfair. As long as he returned the contents, including the vitally important note-book with the phone numbers of Sashok's contacts, and his diary the contents of which were private and intended for nobody's eyes but his own. Let him take also all the idiotic rubbish including the rusty old alarm clock with its customary deafening chimes at the most inappropriate moments, the ladies' training shoe, left foot, and a copy of the British communist newspaper, The Morning Star for the 12th January 1979. And two other weird objects left in the joker's briefcase were the playing cards (just the black ones) and the strange dictionary entitled Diccionario Ecologico Luso-Japones. Sashok had placed all these odds and ends in a Moscow Duty Free bag and now kept a firm grip of them with his left hand as he looked out for the man in the quilted jacket. But what if he'd changed his clothes? How would Sashok recognise him? He did not have a particularly memorable face and if the joker decided to turn up in a different garb, without his quilted jacket, Sashok would not know him from Adam. 'Maybe that was the whole idea?' Sashok thought. 'Draw all the attention to your exotic outfit and nobody will remember your face.' In any case, Sashok had been standing for over half an hour at that lousy suburban line station just outside London, where the Folkestone train and inter-city expresses don't even stop, and gradually became convinced that he had been stood up.

New Cross is a big, chaotic station. How much more convenient it would have been to meet at South Bermondsey, although on the other hand, it would have been essential to avoid the time just before and after a football match. It was at this point that, through an association of ideas, he recalled another strange meeting.

Sashok and his wife were staying at the time in Bermondsey with Anna-Maria's aunt. They did not stay there long, just a few weeks, but Sashok clocked up a lot of journeys to work via this station. And on a couple of occasions he found himself in an awkward situation when crowds of red-faced, roaring passengers squeezed themselves into the carriages. Sashok quickly learned to tell whether Millwall had won or lost, and realised that, in the latter case, it was better to huddle up in the farthest corner of the carriage and avoid all eye contact with the red-faced fans......otherwise anything could happen. On more than one occasion Sashok witnessed a surging maelstrom in the carriage which ended in a brawl. Newspapers mentioned all-out battles between football fans and more often than not these war reports contained references to Millwall. Sashok even developed the almost reflex reaction of scanning the stadium on his approach to the station, wondering if he could expect to be inundated by a flood of dangerous humanity. In which case it might be better to wait for the torrent to subside. But one evening he was obliged to travel into central London on business when he spotted a sizeable group of misbehaving and possibly angry gentlemen, all with beer-bellies and carrying what looked like sticks or spears in their hands. The gentlemen were waving these objects about at the same time as making threatening bellowing noises. The train appeared on the horizon. Of course Sashok could have recalled his youthful, college involvement with track and field events, his super-charged sprints in the four-hundred-metres, and made a dash for it with the real possibility of getting away safely. 'On the other hand,' he thought, 'why should I run when I could just stroll along enjoying the fresh air at a leisurely, dignified pace as befits a respectable representative of the middle classes. There'll be another train along in half an hour and then – fresh air again and there'll be more room in the carriage.'

When Sashok got to the station he found that his platform was almost deserted, there was only one other man there. He was not quite standing and not quite sitting, but was fixed in some sort of impossible pose which evoked vague associations with Rodin's 'Thinker', if you can use this comparison while describing a man who is very drunk and involved in a life-and-death struggle with gravity. Cautiously taking a few steps closer Sashok discovered to his amazement that the man was crying. With one hand he was smearing tears all over his face and in the other had a tight grip on a can of beer; but the can was so large that it would be more appropriate to refer to it as a small barrel. In addition this mournful 'thinker' was pretty big, just over six feet, with shoulders as broad as a barn door and a stomach not much smaller.

This stomach was supported by something resembling a lance that had been broken in half and probably explained why he was able to maintain such a fantastic pose. And the lance, on closer inspection, turned out to be a broken piece of wood from a banner or placard.

Against his better judgement and instinct of self-preservation Sashok moved dangerously close to the giant and was astonished to hear himself saying 'Are you all right?'

How stupid can you be? It was quite obvious that the 'gentleman' was not all right. He looked at Sashok with his huge, tear-stained eyes, stared fixedly at him for what seemed an age, desperately trying to understand what was standing in front of him; but he did not hit Sashok with his stick or even swear at him, just groaned and gestured towards the stadium with his beer can. 'Is he dumb, I wonder,' thought Sashok, but still repeated the question 'Are you sure you're O.K?' intending to make sure the man didn't need an ambulance. In reply the 'thinker' groaned even louder and offered Sashok the remaining contents of his can of beer.

Instinct suggested to Sashok that it would not be wise to refuse this offer or even discuss it. There was only one course of action open to him: he should thank the gentleman nicely, overcome his disgust and take a swig. The disgust was evoked not so much by squeamishness but by his own dislike of the British variant of beer called bitter. He could never understand how anyone could derive any pleasure from drinking this dark, warm and, indeed, slightly bitter drink with an aftertaste of mould. But at that dramatic point of his life he managed to convince himself that bitter was delicious. He took a swig and then smacked his lips as the sign of enjoyment.

When the can of beer had been drunk there was a lot of waving of arms and eloquent mumbling on one side and polite agreement on the other. Then Sashok helped the 'thinker' get onto the train and had to endure the six-minute journey to London, red with embarrassment under the baffled gaze of their fellow-passengers. On London Bridge station, fortunately, his humanitarian mission came to an end: the

Millwall warriors were dashing up and down the platform in search of their absent comrade. On the platform the dumb 'thinker' suddenly sobered up, shook Sashok by the hand so hard that it hurt and said, 'I'm Kevin.' 'I am Sasha', mumbled Sashok.

After that he met Kevin a couple of times on the train and, strange as it might seem, he always recognised Sashok and gave him an encouraging pat on the shoulder, although he could not remember Sashok's name and for some reason addressed him as 'governor.' At such moments, judging by certain outward signs, such as the way his accompanying gang of football fans behaved towards him, Sashok drew the conclusion that Kevin was a very important member of the group and might even have been their unofficial leader.

Now here once again was the railway and the platform on the suburban station not far from Millwall and once again a meeting with a stranger – maybe not such a dangerous meeting, but nevertheless one which aroused vague feelings of alarm.

But the clown apparently did not deign to show up. Sashok was on the point of packing it up and setting off on the long road home via London, and God knows how long that was going to take ('to Rome via Crimea' as the Russians say), when suddenly a powerful, agile and brazen fist grabbed hold of Sashok's Moscow Duty Free bag. A stocky lad in faded jeans and dirty T-shirt examined its contents without paying any attention to Sashok.

'Here, you can't do that!' protested Sashok, speaking Russian.

But at the same time he looked at the gentleman and thought, 'Is this him? It can't be! What a difference clothes can make to a man! He looks like a typical member of the English working class, perhaps a Millwall supporter.'

'Listen, you can't grab things out of people's hands like that,' Sashok said switching to English to be on the safe side.

At this moment the man turned to Sashok and by the surly, malicious and yet familiar look in his small, narrow eyes he recognised a fellow-countryman. But not the one he expected to see.

The stranger in turn was unceremoniously surveying Sashok from head to toe. Finally, he pursed his lips, spat on the platform and said in a typically southern Russian accent,

'Did you come from Moldova recently?'

'Moldova? Are you mad? I've never been to Moldova in my life.'

'Swear to God.'

'Is this some kind of a joke?'

'Don't you believe in God?'

'Me? That's a very personal question. And just who are you, if you don't mind my asking?'

'I'm Lyosha and you're Sasha. Now swear to God.'

'Who gave you permission to talk to me in such a familiar fashion?'

'Is that what I'm doing?

The man calling himself Lyosha, burst out laughing for some reason. Then he suddenly fell silent again, fixed his eyes on Sashok somewhat maliciously and said,

'Swear to God ... please.'

'Well, OK, if you really insist. I give you my solemn oath that never in my life have I set foot in holy, Eastern Orthodox Moldova.... Amen.'

'So why the article about Moldova?'

'Ah, that's what this is all about! You've read my article about Moldovan textiles!'

Lyosha did not contradict the obvious, but just snorted and said,

'Listen, tell me about the mill in Tiraspol.'

'The Tiraspol mill? I don't know anything about it. And as far as what's contained in my article.... I've already forgotten. I don't think the article was all that informative. And in any case, Tiraspol's in the Transdniester region.'

'It's in Moldova,' insisted Lyosha.

'Well, OK, legally speaking.... Now, listen to me, take your hands off me, where are you dragging me to, I'm going nowhere with you!'

The narrow-eyed Lyosha had grabbed hold of Sashok and was dragging him towards the station exit.

'Listen, you dickhead, why didn't you bring my pal's briefcase?' Lyosha said ominously. 'Have you left it at home? Now we will have to sort you out.'

'Wait, I can explain everything,' squealed Sashok.

But the man with the slit eyes was unmoved.

'As for Moldova, you will be held to account for what you've said,' he whispered dragging Sashok further and further on, past a Safeway store, and down a suspicious and foreboding-looking alleyway.

CHAPTER FIVE

Odder and odder

In the rather dirty alleyway behind the supermarket where the narrow-eyed hood had dragged Sasha it was dark, filthy and deserted. But a tough-looking black man, dressed in overalls, was leaning against the wall in a far corner, pulling occasionally on a cigarette. 'This one isn't going to be on my side,' Sasha thought anxiously, 'he'll say 'my lunch break is over'.'

'My lunch break is over!' the black man really did say in English but then immediately switched to Russian. 'How long do you expect me to wait for you, Lyosha. Where do you think you've been? And why have you dragged this old sod here?'

'Client's turned out to be a tricky one,' Lyosha said by way of justification, and holding Sashok all the time in his iron embrace. 'He's having us on'.

'Has he not brought the goods?' with these words the black gentleman came right up to Sasha, threateningly.

'See for yourself,' said Lyosha, handing the black man the Moscow Duty Free bag. The latter rummaged in the bag, all the time muttering away incoherently under his breath.

Just at this point Sashok recovered from the shock enough to squeal out nervously,

'I've brought them, I've brought a lot! I've brought the alarm-clock! And the newspapers! And the dictionary....Luso.....Luso-Japanese. And the cards. In fact, I've brought everything that was in the briefcase.'

The black man, seemingly amazed, stared at Sashok as if he had not expected him to be able to speak.

'And the briefcase, did the sod bring the briefcase?' he said addressing his sidekick.

'You see,' said Sashok, getting anxious, 'there is a problem....'

'I don't understand,' the black man ignored Sashok and went on talking only to Lyosha. 'Where's the briefcase, you oaf?'

'Dynkin,' Lyosha said, 'he hasn't brought the briefcase!'

In the filthy alleyway behind the supermarket there was a sudden tense silence. No one said a word. Then Sashok picked up the meaningful looks being exchanged by Lyosha and the black-skinned Dynkin, and understood he was in serious trouble; the earth spun under Sashok's feet....

At the same time as Sashok was engaged in the unpleasant discussion with Dynkin and his pale-faced friend Lyosha in the New Cross area, back home in Folkestone strange happenings were also taking place. That evening his family was all home early and had sat down for dinner as a threesome.

'I'm a bit worried about Sasha,' said Maggie as she served the smoked salmon which she had bought on offer at the local Sainsbury's. 'And this is a strange business about the briefcase, don't you think?'

'And the gentleman in Russian national costume,' added John. 'It's all a bit weird....'

In eccentric England, naturally, there exist at least a dozen words conveying the meaning 'strange.' Some are neutral, some are positive, but John chose one of the most negative – 'weird'.....Anna-Maria immediately jumped to her husband's defence.

'It wasn't Sasha who acted weird! His reaction was perfectly natural. What would you have done in his place?'

'Well....' John muttered in reply. This word, depending on the intonation and circumstances, can have hundreds if not thousands of different meanings. In this instance it expressed doubt in Sashok's judgement, although in a subtle way of course. Not a doubt really but just a question mark. Nevertheless, Anna-Maria clearly got the sublime message and sulked. Maggie tried to restore the peace by bringing the conversation round to the meal but those assembled around the family table were united only in their appreciation of the green salad. Anna-Maria was a vegan, i.e. an extreme vegetarian. 'I don't eat anybody' she announced with pride, and looked at the pink salmon with scarcely concealed disgust. But her parents, casting sly sideways glances on Anna-Maria's separately prepared dinner, reciprocated the feeling of revulsion.

Vegans refuse categorically and without any exceptions to include in their diet not only meat and fish but also milk, cheese, butter, dairy products in general, and even eggs and honey ('We are against the exploitation of the bees!').

'Bees must not be exploited, but the exploitation of parents, that's ok,' John sometimes would say sarcastically to his wife when Anna-Maria was out of earshot, referring to the fact that expensive nuts, the different kinds of tofu etc. were purchased mainly at his expense, since the young couple's meagre contribution to the household budget would not cover such items. But he would not like to cause offence and kept his mouth shut, looking in horror at the strange-looking dishes which Anna-Maria had prepared ('Weird,' thought John, 'whatever way you look at it, it's weird').

'So this is the stuff you call tofu, isn't it?' John asked as he cast a sideways glance at the enormous sieve which contained something that looked like yellowish porridge.

'Dad, I've already told you that this is quinoa.'

'Tofu is something entirely different; it's a kind of giant mushroom,' Maggie chipped in with an air of superiority.

'What do you mean, mushroom?' exclaimed Anna-Maria, 'Are you being serious? Tofu's made from a kind of soya, a vegetable protein. And it's very nutritious. But quinoa is from Latin-America where it's eaten by the natives. You could call it the 'mother of all grains.'

But Anna-Maria's explanations were interrupted by the door bell.

'That'll be Sasha, he must have forgotten his key again.... I'll go and let him in,' she said, delighted at the unexpectedly early return of her husband. She was astonished when, instead of Sashok, she was confronted by an elegantly turned-out gentleman wearing a tie, and in highly polished, expensive shoes.

In England, it has to be said, it is simply not the done thing to arrive at someone's house without having a previously arranged appointment. It is true that proponents of various religions as well as shameless salesmen, using so-called 'hard-sell' techniques, sometimes overlook this rule, but the reception they receive is always appropriate: in more common households they are abused and chased away like stray dogs and even (what else would you expect?) have something thrown over them in the heat of the moment. While the educated classes (who, in a spirit of classical self-deprecation, sometimes call themselves the chattering class) shower the unfortunate commercial travellers with the full force of their English scorn.

But on this occasion the unbidden guest who rang the bell bore no resemblance whatever to a travelling salesman and even less to an itinerant missionary.

'This is Mr ... er ...' Anna-Maria distractedly attempted to introduce the gentleman to her parents.

'Byenik,' stepped in the guest, bowing politely.

'Mr. Byenik....he's come to see Sasha. It's about the briefcase'.

'About the briefcase?' Maggie blurted out, 'Sasha's gone to meet someone on New Cross station. Wasn't it you?'

'Please accept my sincerest apologies, but I'm afraid Alexander has confused things again. Despite his undoubted intelligence it seems he can be a little absent-minded at times, don't you agree?'

Anna-Maria and her parents were at a loss for something to say in reply.

'We,' the guest continued, 'did originally have an arrangement to meet on New Cross station but then it turned out that I would be returning today from a brief business trip to France, and as I was going to be passing your house, Alexander and I changed our plans. I don't mind waiting, of course, if you have no objection....'

'Can I offer you a cup of tea? Maggie said after a short pause.

Oh! That magical cup of tea! It really is difficult to imagine a situation in an Englishman's life when this tiny porcelain vessel containing a weak drink with no discernible taste, colour or smell, would not be suitable. In situations when Englishmen feel themselves seriously ill-at-ease, do not know what to say, are embarrassed, distracted or upset, the life-saving cuppa comes to the rescue. In everyday situations the 'cup of tea' is usually accompanied by the adjective 'nice.' At first Sashok was a bit nonplussed as to what 'nice' actually meant: 'good' 'pleasant' 'lovely' when applied to tea. But then he realised that the cult of the 'cuppa' penetrates so deeply into the national psyche and is so very particular that it is better not to ask any questions. The love of one's motherland, maternal duty, the necessity to observe the rules of hygiene, all these can be subjects of discussion and even criticism. But two topics are absolutely forbidden: the 'cuppa' and the queen. Or rather they can be discussed, but, have no doubt, many people will think badly of you for it.

Mister Byenik, although a foreigner, gratefully accepted the offer and was shown into the sitting room (in Russian it would be called *gostinaya*, the 'guest room') and so the family enjoyed a certain amount of 'time out' to discuss what to do next. Should they allow the guest to wait till Sashok came home? Heaven alone knew how much longer he would be. Perhaps they should ask Mister what's-his-name (it was a funny name anyway!) to come another day. But no, that would be most impolite. After all Sashok probably had got the time and place wrong, that would be just like him.

Anna-Maria, for the umpteenth time, expressed her regret that Sashok did not possess a mobile phone, but nobody paid any attention to her observation (the expression on John's face asked the question: and who's going to pay for him to have a mobile, might I ask?). And Sashok will never think to use a public phone.

In brief, the decision was taken to get straight to the point with their guest. Maggie was dispatched to the sitting room (on the pretext of offering some biscuits to go with the tea) and soon reported back: it turned out that the stranger had brought Sashok's briefcase with him and hoped to exchange it for his own. Mr Byenik was obviously thinking that Sashok had taken his (Mr Byenik's) briefcase to New Cross....and Maggie could not take it upon herself to persuade him otherwise.

'After all, it's probably best not to overload him with details,' John suggested. 'He and Sashok will sort things out.'

This proposal seemed acceptable to all and it would mean that Mr Byenik would be going away empty-handed. But then something unbelievable happened. The guest came out of the sitting room, where he had been expected to sit quietly until his hosts came for him, put his head round the door and asked if he could use the toilet.

'Please accept my humble excuses' he said, 'but I've come straight from France. It's a long time since I had a chance.....'

'But of course, of course,' John muttered and went off to show Mr Byenik the way.

About ten minutes passed in anxious expectation. John tried to explain something about the state of affairs in the stock-market. Anna-Maria began trying to persuade her parents to sample vegan food, assuring them that they would like it. 'I won't like it,' John answered. 'How do you know you won't like it if you've never tried it? It has such a delicate flavour,' she replied. 'And it's expensive,' Maggie interjected, as ever.

But then the moment arrived when it was impossible to continue the pretence that nothing extraordinary was going on. John glanced meaningfully at his watch, then at the ceiling. Maggie was on the point of opening her mouth to say something, when....

Then events took a totally unexpected turn. A sort of groan could be heard upstairs followed by the sound of a door slamming, then Mr. Byenik came flying down the stairs, shouting wildly. He burst into the dining room brandishing the dishevelled-looking briefcase.

'How did this happen?' he said reproachfully. 'You've been telling me a load of lies! It turns out that my briefcase has been here all the time and not at New Cross or wherever! It's been sitting quietly in this house.... That's how you English behave!'

'We ... I ... Sasha....' the confused hosts squeaked in their discordant voices.

'But you can't begin to imagine what this briefcase means to me!' sobbed Byenik, 'if you must know, it was a present from my late brother.'

'But just a minute,' John said, suddenly realising what was going on, 'how did you find it? You must have gone into one of the upstairs bedrooms and searched the place!'

'And do you know how my brother died? How he suffered? And you, Mrs Tutov, what do you know about all this?'

'But....'

'Never mind 'but!' Just have a look at what your Alexander has done!'

And Byenik placed the briefcase which Sashok had destroyed in front of the family so everybody could see it.

'First he mixed up the briefcases then shot on to the train and didn't even turn round. Don't you recognise my description of your beloved Sashok? Come now! Don't you know that I'm speaking the truth? And you tried to fool me! For a miserable little briefcase! You sit here stuffing yourselves with salmon and all these ... substances (Byenik looked at the quinoa).... Insensitive people without any conscience!'

Graphically brandishing the tattered briefcase, Mr Byenik virtually sang his last words and finished them somewhere on a top A. The whole family maintained a stunned silence.

'To sum up, then,' the guest continued in a different and unexpectedly hoarse tone of voice, 'there's just no hope of repairing this briefcase. It would of course be possible to patch it up a bit for forty or fifty pounds, but it would never look as good. So this is my suggestion: I'll take both. I'll use one for work, and I'll put the other away somewhere.' Byenik looked around the room and then said,

'Yes, there, I'll keep it on my mantlepiece.... Yes.... As a memorial to my brother.'

'Now hang on! You're being unfair,' Anna-Maria suddenly spoke up.

'And is it fair to snatch other people's things?' retorted Byenik. 'And is it OK to tear up the gifts of a late brother who died in such agony? No, it is not OK!' With these words he brought out the second briefcase from somewhere behind his back and, opening it up over the table, proceeded to empty the contents right onto the plates of food. Here were Sashok's newspapers, booklets and notebooks. 'I don't need this rubbish,' he muttered.

When Byenik left the house nobody said anything for a long time. Then John spoke up,

'How very odd…. Do you think this man is Russian?'

'I don't know,' said Maggie, 'when I was seeing him out he was muttering words which sounded really weird…. Let me see if I can remember them…. 'Khle-balni-niki-ra-zi-nu-li' or something like that…. Do you know what it means, Anna-Maria?'

'No,' Anna-Maria answered sullenly, 'I don't even think it's Russian. Russian is a much more beautiful language!'

Meanwhile, an hour and a half's journey from Folkestone, near New Cross, in a dirty stinking alleyway three men (one black and two white) were squatting down, engaged in what appeared to be a calm exchange of views and opinions.

'This has gone on long enough,' one of the white men said to the other almost in a whisper. 'Dynkin doesn't need your rubbish. He needs your briefcase. It's a keep-sake of our dead brother,' said Lyosha pointing in the direction of the black man. 'Memories are sacred. So you will have to deliver, agreed?

Sashok nodded, or at least, attempted to make a movement with his head.

'He'll bring it, Dynkin, he'll bring it, like I said. He understands, he is not retarded,' Lyosha concluded.

'I'll bring it,' Sashok finally managed to say, 'I'll bring both briefcases tomorrow without fail, if that's the way it has to be.'

'There's a clever boy!' said Lyosha, pleased with what he had just heard. 'And just to add a little encouragement we'll charge you fifty quid a day, counting from today.'

After these words had been spoken Dynkin took the rusty old alarm-clock out and, with a single deft conjuror's touch, wound it up. The clock started to tick, disgustingly and loudly, filling the whole alleyway with its creaking sinister sound.

CHAPTER SIX

A fellow countryman from Hell

There was a minute and a half to go before the arrival of the Charing Cross train and already the muffled sound of the electric locomotive could be heard from the direction of Dover's white cliffs. The passengers on Folkestone Central station sprang to life and crowded up to the yellow line at the platform edge. Sashok also moved towards the yellow line. He had a Debenhams plastic bag in his hand and now, that he no longer had a briefcase, it contained all his belongings. Suddenly someone patted him on the shoulder. Turning round, Sashok expected to see Philip, a charming old gentleman, a former architect, who sometimes had business to attend to in London. Or it might have been Harry, the burglar (officially unemployed) who, Sashok's family believed, had already cleared their house out four times and had become more and more familiar when he met them face-to-face. But no, it was neither Philip nor Harry, but a certain gentleman who was dressed, like the majority of the passengers, in a grey, baggy, nondescript suit. But it was difficult not to notice something else: the two briefcases which the gentleman was carrying. One of them he gripped firmly in his right hand, and the other was slung across his left shoulder.

'Greetings, Alexander. What kind of weather do you call this?' the stranger suddenly said in Russian and as soon as Sashok heard his voice he recognised it. He also recognised the two briefcases.

There was no doubt about it; this was the same mad joker who, a couple of weeks earlier, had interrupted the peaceful flow of Sashok's life. On that occasion, it is true, he had been wearing an absurd padded jacket, a cap with ear-flaps and, on his feet he had felt boots and galoshes. 'How clothes can change a man,' thought Sashok, amazed. 'I would have walked right past him and not recognised him.'

On his first appearance this character had played a game with the two briefcases; he had confused Sashok and placed him in a ridiculous situation at work. But now he got also mixed up in a dreadful business with some Russian gangsters whose boss was a black man called Dynkin, who spoke the Solntsevo-Mytishinsky dialect of Russian without any accent. Sashok was in absolutely no doubt that he had stumbled into some mafia plot. He thought the most probable explanation was that the briefcase which had been thrust into his hands must have contained a double bottom which hid something the gangsters considered very valuable. For example, it could have been cocaine, or money or compromising material of one sort or another. Heaven alone knew why the gang has chosen Sashok for their nefarious games. And then they wanted to use him without his knowledge (keeping him in the dark, as it's called). Or perhaps, the whole episode was just a matter of chance and coincidence. One of them just happened to spot Sashok – a fellow countryman with a briefcase similar to the one they had at hand. And so, on the spur of the moment, they decided to exploit Sashok. That seemed a very plausible explanation.

Then the bandits wanted to get their stuff back but, obviously, had split into two groups or some problem had come up between them. Sashok would have preferred to report the whole affair to the police. But what could he tell them? 'This Russian black man promised to poke his side-kick's eyes out and cut off his balls. At first he didn't even look at me. And when he finally did, it gave me the shivers.'

But is it really against the law to give someone the shivers? No, he certainly could not report this to the police and he would never be able to explain the situation to Anna-Maria either, let alone her parents.

And then, just as Sashok was feeling on the brink of total despair, that same clown who had caused all his troubles, turned up again on Folkestone Central. 'The start of another game,' Sashok said to himself, horrified, 'the swine has shown me both briefcases.....the bait he's fishing with.'

And then Sashok said,

'So, it was you who came to our house when I was out? You're Mr Byenik!'

'Of course I am. Who else did you think I was?'

'And you took both briefcases!'

'Well, it can't be denied, can it? OK, come on, get onto the train.'

And with these words he shoved Sashok into the carriage. Then he settled down next to him.

'I'm amazed at these English trains,' Byenik went on in an animated voice. 'Who would have thought we'd be travelling like this in this day and age?'

As Sashok could not think of anything to say in reply to this observation, Byenik continued his own monologue. When he had exhausted the theme of the state of the railways in Britain, he moved smoothly on to agriculture.

'Look, look,' he said, pointing to the pastoral landscape flashing past the carriage windows, 'look how many sheep they've got feeding everywhere. Why do they need so many? You couldn't eat them all in a whole lifetime! Sheep are a kind of cult animal with the English, don't you agree? And they tend to behave like them as well. I've watched them on the train or the Tube.....they never think of moving down to the middle of the carriage but always crowd around the door. Like sheep!'

Then he let out a forced guffaw and prodded Sashok in the ribs.

But Sashok was miles away. Eight days earlier, returning from a meeting with Dynkin and his side-kick Lyosha, he started to give his family an ear-bashing for handing over the briefcase to the stranger without getting anything in return. But his relations would have none of it. His mother-in-law maintained that it was Sashok who was to blame for getting involved in a silly game with... what was his name? And wasn't Sashok the one who had destroyed someone else's property? And who got everything mixed up by forgetting the place where they were supposed to meet with Mr Byenik?'

'I didn't get anything mixed up,' Sashok was about to say, but bit his tongue. He did not want to start talking about the Russian gangsters and their veiled but frightening threats. 'And,' he thought dejectedly, 'they won't believe me anyway, and if they did they would get into such a state that they would have to call an ambulance.'

To think that just two weeks ago Sashok's life seemed uneventful and even humdrum. In three years seven months and about eighteen days he and Anna-Maria would have finally saved up enough money for the deposit on a house of their own. It was true, however, that the fateful day kept on receding into the future. In theory they should have been putting £250 away per month, but in practice there were months when they managed less than £200. In fact there were times when they saved absolutely nothing. There was a period of a whole three months when they had to forget about putting anything away as Sashok was out of work. But now he and his wife had come to a firm agreement: they would save £175 per month without fail, come hell or high water. Annie even detailed their expenses on a piece of paper. At work Sashok, apart from his sandwich and a drink at lunch time, would allow himself just one cup of tea from the vending machine. But only one! And the rest was in the same spirit and it was, of course, a boring existence. Even going to the theatre or the cinema depended on the kindness of their parents who sometimes asked them to come too. But the repertoire was as you might expect: old-fashioned musicals like Les Miserables and dreary family comedies. So boring! But never mind, Sashok cheered himself up, the mortgage will set us free, we'll buy our own flat or a little house with a garden and then everything will be OK. True, everyone he knew who had already completed the magical transition to home ownership, warned him that a 25-year mortgage would be a millstone round his neck, a veritable prison for a Russian spirit. But people like this couldn't understand, or had forgotten, what it meant to live as a hanger-on in an English family. Roll on freedom!

But now, thanks to this living reminder of his homeland who was now sitting next to him on the train and talking a load of rubbish, everything had gone pear-shaped. Sashok was particularly upset when he thought of the effect it was having on Anna-Maria. He remembered how touchingly she would poke her tongue out as she tried to draw up their expenses, how she secretly saved by skipping her lunches so that she could buy him a Russian-language newspaper or some French aftershave or something else. But she would also give Sashok a bit of a rough ride if he as much as bought himself an extra cup of coffee which had not been budgeted for or treated one of his colleagues to one. She would always show her unhappiness in the English, not the Russian, way: her lips would tighten and she would become all formality and politeness.

'Hey, Sasha,' said Byenik suddenly interrupting Sashok's reverie, 'what is the matter with you today? Why are you sulking? I agree that things haven't turned out very fair for you: I've got two briefcases and you haven't even got one, just that awful plastic bag. But if I give you your briefcase back I'll be left with this broken one. And as you can see I've done my best to stick it all together again. You know if I try to get it repaired properly, I'll be looking at no change out of a hundred quid.'

'How do you work that out? It only cost sixty brand new and you're talking about a hundred to get it repaired?' asked Sashok.

'I agree, it's crazy, but it's always like that in England. Surely you've noticed.'

'I couldn't care now anyway. I'm probably four hundred in debt by now.'

'Who to?'

'To some Afro-Russian....'

Byenik's jaw dropped.

'Not Dynkin, by any chance?'

'Ah, so you know him?' exclaimed Sashok triumphantly. 'I thought so!'

'The fact that I know him is hardly surprising. But that *you* know him – that, my friend is not so good.'

Byenik suddenly changed. His jocular expression seemed to evaporate and Sashok found himself looking at a very worried and serious man.

And this man was now deep in thought. Then he suddenly jumped up, took his leave of Sashok and moved to another carriage, taking both briefcases with him. 'Well, that's a bit odd,' Sashok thought absent-mindedly. But a few minutes later Byenik returned and settled down on the seat next to him again. Had he had a change of mind, or what?

'Alexander,' he said in a serious voice, 'Listen to me very carefully. This Dynkin is a terrible man. You won't find a gangster as terrible as he is.... If you get mixed up with him.... You're done for. Pay up as soon as possible just to get shot of him.'

'Where will I find the money?'

'Take out a loan.'

'But nobody will give me a loan. My credit rating's ......zero.'

'Bullshit! Listen, if necessary, I'll give you the money...well, lend it to you. How much did you say? Four hundred? That's less than six hundred greenbacks. That's not much, really.'

'Thank you, but Dynkin wants both briefcases, that's why he's turned the meter on. At fifty quid a day.'

This news was such a shock to Byenik that he fell silent for a long time and even covered his face with his hands.

'What does he want both for?' he finally asked in a whisper.

'I think it's because he can't be sure which one contains....'

'Contains what?'

'Whatever it is you're hiding in them.'

'Who's hiding something? Me?' Byenik suddenly burst out laughing. Ah, now I see.... You thought there's some sort of dope sewn into it.'

'Or money. Or even....'

'Oh, I get it! You're wrong but I can see where you're coming from and I like the way you are thinking. No, Sasha, this business may be a bit more tricky for you than you think.... But I'll try to get you out of this shit. Today I'll scratch your back and tomorrow you'll scratch mine.'

'Well, yes, but I don't know....'

'You just try and get away from this Dynkin. Don't agree to anything he might tempt you with. Promise?'

'Well, OK, I promise.'

'Swear it!'

'OK then, I swear to God.'

Byenik turned away, thrust his right hand into his inside pocket, rooted about for a few seconds and then brought out a wad of £50 notes.

'Here, take this,' he said. 'There's four hundred and fifty quid there. Just in case that bastard suddenly tops it up by another fifty. And take this briefcase, the damaged one. Give it to him and let's hope he chokes on it! I will charge you another fifty for the briefcase so you'll owe me five hundred all in all. The interest will be eighteen percent per annum. If necessary I'll find you a little part-time job. There's a need here for a translator. What are you like with military terminology?'

'Well I'm no specialist, but if I did a bit of swotting up....'

'And I've also been asked to find somebody who can work in tourism. Could you be a tour guide, say, around the historic pubs of Kent? You could work off the debt.'

'That's fine.... But what if Dynkin demands the other briefcase?' asked Sashok, nervously extending his hand to take the money.

'Just let him try!' said Byenik thrusting the notes into Sashok's palm and squeezing his fingers so much that it hurt. 'Just let the bastard try!'

Byenik's eyes flashed with a kind of infernal fire.

'Yes, that's the term, that's what they call it in Russian – *adskiy* – infernal,' thought Sashok as he put the money away in his pocket.

CHAPTER SEVEN

Dynkin the Terrible

A black Land Rover with opaque windows was standing by the exit from Hither Green station on Wednesday, at one fifteen in the afternoon. The time and place had been suggested to Sashok for a meeting by Lyosha on the instructions, it should be assumed, of his boss, Dynkin the black man. Sashok was worried at first. How would he manage to get there on a working day? But then, with his head in a kind of spin, he went to see his stern boss Mr Singh (nicknamed Sinyukha) and told him a fib about an unbearable toothache and the need to see a dentist urgently. Sashok, as we know, was an unskilled liar (and he considered this deficiency his great weakness), and on this occasion, as usual, he went as red as a beetroot. But, as he had been holding a handkerchief to his cheek for some time and was rubbing it for all he was worth, his blushing went virtually unnoticed. In the spirit of overcoming moral inhibitions Sashok calmed himself down by reasoning that the meeting with Dynkin & Co. could be fairly compared to a visit to the dentist or even two visits. Or even the removal of a nerve or the extraction of two wisdom teeth. And, possibly, having his gum cut in addition. Besides, Sashok remembered that the previous spring, he really had suffered with his teeth but was too timid to ask for time off.

'This can be in lieu of that time,' he thought.

To Sashok's amazement Sinyukha believed him immediately. He just muttered,

'Try to get back as soon as possible.'

'That was easy,' Sashok thought, somewhat surprised at himself. 'Like this I'll soon master this proud art and tell fine fibs on every occasion.'

Sashok had been whizzing past Hither Green station many times on the Ramsgate express, but it was the first time he had actually set foot on the platform there, having travelled from London Bridge in fifteen minutes on a half-empty train. In comparison with the cattle-class inter-city trains, the suburban one with its automatic doors appeared to Sashok to be a modern and even elegant form of transport. The platform at Hither Green also looked not too bad with its rather attractive awning. But then to reach the exit he had to walk through a long gloomy tunnel lit only by a deathly glimmer.

'This could be a road to a mortuary,' thought Sashok, but then he suddenly realised: these thoughts were the result of the impending meeting with Dynkin. This frightening prospect was the reason why everything seemed draped in gloomy shadows. The mere thought of it put a knot in Sashok's stomach.

The unpleasant feeling got even stronger when he saw a smart black car which had impudently mounted the pavement by the exit from the station into the town. Sashok remembered what his wise class mate Gavrilov taught him: at moments like this the most important thing was not to lose one's head. Don't let your imagination run riot, act intuitively, naturally and rely on basic instincts, he said.

'Instincts, engage!' was the inner command Sashok gave himself and walked manfully towards the Land Rover. But the doors of the wretched vehicle were locked and through the smoky glass windows absolutely nothing could be seen. Sashok tugged at both handles on one side of the car, before moving round to the other side. But to no avail.

'Perhaps, they've gone to have a bite, or nipped out to the shops,' he thought.

But Sashok was wrong. The gentlemen who had been waiting in the car were still inside and, evidently, were taking advantage of the situation to have a look at Sashok close-up or to tease him and make him nervous. One way or another, the door suddenly burst open, a black hand emerged, festooned with gold bracelets and rings, and beckoned to him imperiously, inviting him to get in.

'The best form of defence is attack, and when you're attacking things are not so frightening,' thought Sashok, remembering Gavrilov's words of wisdom at the same time as he settled down onto the back seat of the Land Rover, alongside Dynkin, and then immediately went onto the attack.

'Do you think I've got all the time in the world? Are you playing some kind of game with me, or what? I can't believe it: you've been studying me, watching me from behind your tinted windows!'

'What's the matter with him?' Dynkin asked Lyosha who was sitting on the front seat behind the wheel. 'Is he high or something?'

'The guy's just nervous,' replied Lyosha philosophically.

'I'll have something to be nervous about with Sinyukha's wondering where I am,' said Sashok. 'He almost didn't let me come here.'

'What is he talking about? Who the Hell is this Sinyukha?' Dynkin asked Lyosha.

'Haven't a clue,' he replied.

'He's my boss. His surname's Singh,' said Sashok.

'So Sinyukha is something like a nick-name then?'

'Yes, that's what we call him when he is not listening in. Trust me, he is a terrifying character!'

'You tell the client that he shouldn't worry. We'll deal with Sinyukha,' Dynkin said, addressing his side-kick again.

And Lyosha said, in an irritatingly nasal voice,

'Don't you worry about it, Sasha, we'll deal with Sinyukha.'

'Deal with him? In what way?' said Sashok, 'You don't understand.... He's a frightening man. More frightening than any gangster....'

'I said we would sort things out. We either come to some agreement with him. Or else....' Dynkin was getting angry.

'Do you hear? We'll sort Sinyukha out, one way or another,' echoed Lyosha his boss's words.

'Why go to all this trouble? Leave him alone! After all, I brought you the briefcase, didn't I? Now the matter's closed,' Sashok said in a confident voice.

Lyosha reached over the front seat, took hold of the briefcase and gave it to Dynkin. The latter looked inside, felt around and immediately gave it back to Lyosha, who hurriedly got out of the car and carried it off somewhere. He did not come back for probably about ten minutes. Meanwhile Sashok had time to chat about the weather, about the strange habits people have, about Mr Singh's foul temper and even about the dangers of a vegan diet. But Dynkin maintained a stubborn silence and just smoked, spitting periodically out of the window and coughing. Finally, Lyosha came back, said nothing but just gave his boss a meaningful look. They exchanged looks for a long time ('they must have a secret sign language of their own' thought Sashok), then Dynkin closed his eyes and leaned back in his seat as if he was about to fall asleep. And Lyosha said,

'Bad news, comrade. The briefcase is ruined. It'll cost at least fifty quid to get it repaired. And you've already got four hundred on the meter. That makes a total of four hundred and fifty.'

'Here you are,' Sashok said unperturbed and nonchalantly handed Lyosha the envelope which he had prepared earlier. The gangster opened it, counted the notes and muttered,

'Where did you get the money?'

The black man Dynkin opened one eye.

'Oh, it's nothing! Just six hundred greenbacks, peanuts!' Sashok answered.

At that moment Dynkin opened the other eye and whispered to Lyosha,

'Now I'm going to cut your buttons off and the rest as well!'

'Hang on, Boss, don't get so upset, we'll sort it out' Lyosha was now getting fidgety on the front seat.

But Sashok decided that he had had enough.

'So if you have no objection I will bid you farewell, gentlemen,' he said and was just about to open the door, get out and make his way back to the office. But then something happened which was to recur in Sashok's nightmares till the end of his life. With unbelievable agility Lyosha half jumped, half flew across the seat and viciously slammed the door shut, giving Sashok a nasty bang on his arm and knee. With the same lightening speed he then returned to the driver's seat and pressed something there and all of a sudden all the doors were locked. Sashok squeezed back into the corner and began rubbing his injured knee. 'So much for relying on natural instincts, I shouldn't have been so cheeky.... Now they're going to teach me a lesson,' was the thought that flashed through his mind.

Dynkin opened his mouth and let forth a tirade of invective, swear words and curses. But he was so articulate, so theatrical, and the combinations of half-forgotten, exotic Russian expressions were so original and unusual that Sashok, even in his disturbed state of mind, could not suppress a certain admiration. And the invective was once more directed at Lyosha and could thus be ignored as having absolutely nothing to do with Sashok. But Dynkin dispelled the illusion when he said, 'Tell your client, blockhead, that there's no need for him to hurry as we haven't come to an agreement yet.'

'Listen, comrade,' Lyosha replied submissively, 'what's the hurry? And as for the money.....well, we can come to some arrangement. For example you could work the debt off.'

'In what capacity could I work for you?' Sashok asked.

'I don't really know. What are you like at military translations?'

'Military translations? Not all that good....limited experience.'

'And if you swotted it up?'

'If I swotted it up then perhaps I could.'

'Tell him we'd deduct it from the meter,' Dynkin butted in.

'We'll deduct it from the meter. We'll let you work off your debt, you could pay us back and then start earning for yourself,' Lyosha said in his nasal, sing-song voice.

'Tell him he'll be a rich man,' Dynkin added for some reason this time with Georgian accent. But Sashok had a clear memory of Byenik's commandment: don't be taken in by his blandishments and under no circumstances enter into any agreements or strike any deals with him. So he decided to stick to the path he had chosen and put all the blame on Mr Singh.

'No, gentlemen, I can't take on any more work without Mr Singh's permission. You must understand that.'

'It seems to me that he's treating you like a gofer, this Sinyukha of yours,' Lyosha had obviously decided to goad him a bit.

'What can I do about it?' answered Sashok, sighing plaintively. 'I've got to make a living.'

'Well to hell with this Sinyukha. Who is he? We're tougher guys than him.'

'Well, I don't know, I don't know,' Sashok groaned.

'We'll sort him out in half a second, you'll see.'

'We'll talk about it when you do. But now let me out.' said Sashok.

At this point Dynkin joined in the conversation again.

'I'll roast you alive,' he said, as usual addressing Lyosha.

But these indirect threats for some reason ceased to scare Sashok.

'Come on, come on, open it up!' He said in a commanding tone of voice.

'OK,' Dynkin suddenly agreed, 'Let him go. But he's got to tell us first where he got the money from.'

'Where from? My wife's parents lent it to me!' Sashok said without batting an eyelid.

'Tell him,' Dynkin retorted, 'that we won't let him go until he tells us the truth.'

Sashok was plunged into painful thoughts. Should he give Byenik away? Or should he try to spin a more intricate yarn which the gangsters might believe?

'Pity I haven't had much practice at lying yet,' he thought.

For the next few moments there was a tense silence.

'Confession lessens the guilt,' Lyosha said sternly. 'Come on, comrade; get it off your chest. Tell us the truth and it'll be a load off your mind.'

Then, after a brief pause, carefully, as if he were dipping his toe in the water, he asked,

'Perhaps it's Sinyukha's money?'

'Sinyukha's!' exclaimed Sashok, astonished, 'He wouldn't lend a penny even to his own mother.'

They were silent a bit longer. Then Lyosha turned sharply to Dynkin and, with a gesture of abject submission, exclaimed, 'It's a no-brainer! If Byenik's not behind all this then I'm a Chinaman!'

In reply the black-skinned Russian came out with such monstrously foul expressions and terrifying threats that Sashok wished he could block up his ears. Then, all of a sudden, as if somebody had pressed a remote control button, Dynkin broke off in the middle of a lengthy obscenity and said, in a totally different voice, 'Let the client go. It's time we were off.'

The levers of the Land Rover's locking mechanism made a loud clunking noise and the door opened, revealing Sashok's road to freedom.

'Good bye, comrade,' Lyosha shouted as he walked away, 'we'll see you soon.'

All the way back to the office Sashok thought about how he had perhaps been a little harsh in the things he said about Mr Singh. OK, it's true; he does not give the impression of being a generous man. In fact he is a bit tight, but then he is saddled with a mortgage and has kids to bring up and all the rest. But then to look at Sashok in the office, with his sandwiches and just one cup of tea per day, anyone would think that he was a skinflint, too. Then Sashok remembered the other painful details of what had happened. and, completing the circle, his thoughts returned to Sinyukha. He suddenly felt himself go cold deep inside. 'What if they really do 'sort things out' with Mr Singh? And what exactly did they mean by that expression?'

Sashok was so engrossed in his thoughts that he did not notice how he made it back to Century Building. He did not at first spot the man in the light-grey, doubled breasted suit walking up and down right by the entrance. It was only when he had already walked past him that, turning round, he took another look at the painfully familiar gentleman. At that same moment he detected his own beloved briefcase in the gentleman's hand. There was no room for the slightest doubt; this was Byenik, the man who was transformed almost beyond recognition with every change of clothes.

'How did you find out where I worked?' Sashok exclaimed in an agitated voice.

'How did I find out?' answered the clown in a self-satisfied tone, 'from your political mother, when we were drinking tea together.'

'What do you mean, 'political mother'? Are you having a laugh?'

'You should study foreign languages! In Spanish the term for mother-in-law is 'political mother.' I pop over to Spain quite frequently these days. I like it there, you see.'

'He is lying through his teeth and talking nonsense,' thought Sashok angrily. He decided not to say anything to Byenik about how Lyosha and Dynkin guessed his role in re-financing Sashok's debt.

'I can't spare the time to talk to you now; my boss is expecting me,' Sashok said sternly and made a bee-line for the lift.

'Just hold on a minute,' Byenik said, chasing after him, 'have you forgotten that you owe me a lot of money?'

The memory of the money cooled Sashok's temper.

'I'll pay you back.' he muttered sheepishly.

'When? Bear in mind that I can't wait long. And tell me, how's the meter running with Dynkin? Have you severed your connection with him?'

'Sort of....'

'Really? Well done! Who would have thought.... You're a lucky son-of-a-bitch. Good I was able to help.'

'Thanks,' said Sashok, looking at the ground.

'And don't worry about the money too much, you can work it off. You said you were good at military translation, didn't you?'

'No I didn't! What's this obsession everyone's got with military translations?'

'Never mind. You can work as a guide, can't you?'

'I think I can.'

'Excellent. Tomorrow morning. Early. At seven o'clock. You will meet someone on your station, Folkestone Central. You'll be working for a lady. She is rich. One of the new Russians, if you take my meaning.'

'Impossible! I have to go to work tomorrow.'

'Don't worry about that. Say you're sick. Otherwise you might never have a chance like this again.'

'And do you realise what my boss will do to me?'

'He won't do anything. I'll sort things out with him, I promise.'

'You better sort things out first. Everyone's good at sorting things out from a distance.'

And then Sashok fell silent. The doors of the lift opened and out walked Mr Singh. He totally ignored Sashok and walked straight up to Byenik. They walked over to one side and began a friendly, confidential conversation as if they had known each other for ages. Sashok could not believe his eyes. He could just about make out a few words of what they were saying, but he clearly heard Byenik use the term 'military terminology.' 'Military translation again!' Sashok said, amazed. At that moment the lift doors opened again and Sashok decided that there was no point hanging around and it was time to go up to the sixth floor. But just as he was about to step into the lift Sinyukha shouted to him,

'Mr Tutov, there's no need for you to come into work tomorrow. I'm aware of the situation.'

CHAPTER EIGHT

A nice kind of kidnapping – With a bad ending

In vain Sashok hoped that his adventures were at an end. No such luck: somebody in a heavenly chancellery, or wherever the balance sheet of our daily lives is drawn up, decided he hadn't had enough yet: 'Oh, no brother, that won't do. There's obviously been a misunderstanding if you've got away from the gangsters' Land Rover without any wounds to body or soul. You are going to get some more of the same!'

So at the end of a less than productive day's work in Century Building (Sashok at the time was editing an extremely boring article on the Latvian energy industry), as soon as he ran out onto London Bridge, wondrous things started happening to him again.

Something suddenly separated him from the crowd wending its way to the station. For a second it even seemed to him that he was somehow soaring through the air. He found the feeling an entirely pleasant one until he realised that he was being hemmed in on both sides by two hefty young men in black jackets. With their lantern jaws and small but watchful eyes the pair looked like twins. And they were not Slavs; they were more like Anglo-Saxons or Germans and could have been ex-rugby players, or something similar. They practically carried him in a predetermined direction, easily parting the crowd as they did so. At the slightest attempt to tear away or alter the course of this trajectory he felt the grip of steel fingers on both sides ... careful, or it'll hurt!

'I'll have to shout out as loud as I can and make people turn round and understand that this is no joke and that I'm being kidnapped!' he thought, but he did not manage to derive any practical conclusion from this supposition because the 'rugby players' dragged him to a bus-stop where a picturesque crowd of people were having a gentle argument with the stern conductor of a double-decker red bus. 'Full up inside,' he insisted tetchily. But the crowd (white, black and yellow faces) looked sceptical as if they did not believe him but stopped short of arguing the call. Sashok and his escort found themselves right in front of the conductor who nervously tugged on the cord to signal the driver to move off, but the bus could not move. The bridge was, as usual at that time of day, at a complete standstill. 'I've been kidnapped,' Sashok said in a scarcely audible voice so that the only person who heard him was the conductor. The rugby players' fingers dug into Sashok beneath his ribs so that he found it difficult to breathe. The conductor turned his head and said bad-temperedly 'I'm telling you, governor, there isn't even any standing room. And I'm not in the mood for any more of your jokes!'

'You don't understand! I have been kidnapped!' Sashok asserted a little more insistently this time but this was followed by an unbearable pain in his ribs.

'Sorry, not even upstairs,' shrugged the conductor.

Overcoming the pain, Sashok was finally able to take in enough breath to let out an appropriate yell, but the bus suddenly pulled away only to be replaced by a ginormous and unnaturally long limousine with blacked-out windows, (such as those in which VIPs and nouveau riche obsessed by their own importance travel). Either from astonishment or from pain, Sashok missed the opportunity to shout out. The rear door burst open, one of the 'rugby players' dived onto the back seat, dragging Sashok with him, and a second, just like you see the police doing in a TV drama, pushed his head down and Sashok was sucked into the bowels of the limo, which immediately pulled away.

Well, pull away it did but it did not get very far. It got snarled up in an enormous tailback at London Bridge.

'Rush hour, I'm afraid. We'll be stuck here for ages,' the man sitting with his back to Sashok (where, in a normal car, the driver would be sitting) politely explained. But this VIP limousine (a 'stretched limo' as Sashok remembered they were called) was so spacious that you could stretch your legs out fully and still not reach the gentleman sitting in front, nor even the partition separating the driver from the passenger. Now Sashok, remembering Hollywood films, expected to find a TV set and fridge and mini-bar or something like that. But instead of a TV there was a computer screen which the gentleman was checking from time to time. In the dimness it was difficult to make him out, but from the man's bearing and his resonant Oxford accent, Sashok made the deduction that this was a gentleman of high social standing.

'I must offer you my apologies,' said the gentleman with an expansive hand gesture which suggested a certain disgust at the vulgar choice of car, the 'rugby players' and the awkwardness of the situation itself, 'but a certain unforeseen and urgent circumstance has arisen which has made it imperative for us to communicate with you directly, Mr Tutov.'

'Are you the police?' Sashok asked, hopefully. (He knew himself that he was clutching at straws: who ever heard of the police using VIP limos? They have to economise as well, they haven't got enough paper or paper-clips even.)

'Not exactly, Mr Tutov, not exactly,' said the man of breeding (Oh, that incomparable English expression: not exactly!). 'But you're not that far off'.

He then paused for a while and said,

'Mr Tutov, before we go any further I would like you to call home to say that you have been delayed. The last thing I want to do is to cause you any domestic troubles.'

'But I don't have a mobile!'

'That's not a problem, Mr Tutov. You can use mine. On condition, of course, that you do not attempt to go into too many details'.

Sashok realised that he needed to hear Anna-Maria's voice (or even John's or Maggie's) so much that he would have agreed to anything for that phone call. Also there was a hope that his wife would detect something in his voice which would make her suspect that something right out of the ordinary had happened to him. And, anyway, what did 'going into too many details' really mean? Did it include, for instance, shouting into the receiver 'I've been kidnapped?' Would that come under the definition or not? Maybe not literally. On the other hand these people could strangle or cripple without bothering with interpretations. Sashok cast a sideways glance at the two heavies sitting motionless on either side of him, like robots. 'They don't even look like they're breathing,' he thought.

Then he said aloud,

'I promise…'

And then, remembering Lyosha, quickly added,

'I swear by almighty God.'

The grand personage politely nodded and fished out from somewhere beneath the computer a strange-looking mobile phone with funny buttons.

'Tell me what your home phone number is.'

'Zero, One, three, zero, three, seven….'

Sashok had the feeling that the fine gentleman knew his phone number by heart; his fingers flew over the mobile's keypad. When he had pushed all the buttons he handed the phone to Sashok and … what a shock! It was so heavy that Sashok almost dropped it. He was listening to the tone and thinking hard how he should conduct the conversation with Anna-Maria so that she would understand that something was not right. Then he heard a familiar voice.

'Hello,' yelled Sashok in a maniacally joyful tone, 'Anna-Maria, is that you?'

'Why are you shouting? Of course it's me.'

'I'd like to speak to Anna-Maria.'

'What's the matter with you, Sash? What is going on? You never phone me from work! What's happened?'

'I'm held up at the office. Can you hear me?' Sashok yelled at the top of his voice. 'I repeat, I ... am ... held... up... at... the office!'

'Sash, there's no need to bellow like this.... I can hear you all right.' Anna-Maria also suddenly started shouting. 'Sash, what's happened? Are you sure you are all right?'

'I've got some work to do urgently! Yes, yes, I've got an urgent job again. I'll spell it out....'

'What do you mean by 'again'? It's never happened before. And you yourself have always said that Mr Singh chases everyone out after six.'

'I've got a lot of work again,' Sashok persisted, 'I've got seventy articles, three thousand files, ten thousand couriers. And we're also celebrating his daughter's birthday.'

'Daughter? Whose daughter?'

'Mr Singh's, of course, who else's.'

'You said his children were all grown up and his wife's fifty!'

'Even two daughters in fact.... They had twins.... That sort of thing happens nowadays.'

'Sasha, forgive my asking, but ... have you been drinking?'

'Oh, just a tiny bit. We're having a little party. A couple of colleagues have got things to celebrate. It's Vugar's birthday. You know Vugar, don't you? And then Tsveta.... Remember Tsveta? She's completely cured now!'

'Cured? Of what?'

'I'm telling you: completely, totally cured! It all happened in one day, isn't it a mystery? Mr Singh is pretty much dancing and singing!'

'Mr Singh dancing?'

'I'm exaggerating a bit. He's here now, right beside me, he sends his regards. Would you like a word with him?'

Taking no notice of Anna-Maria who was trying to say that she had no wish to speak to Mr Singh, Sashok attempted to hand the phone to the member of nobility. But the latter clearly didn't want to join in the game and angrily pushed the phone aside.

Anna-Maria was clearly annoyed.

'I don't understand what's happened to you,' she said drily. 'I don't have the time to play silly games. I'm off to a seminar on ecology.... If you get home before me the keys will be with the neighbours.'

'Listen....' Sashok shouted, but too late. Anna-Maria had already hung up.

Sashok was morosely silent for a minute. His Excellency took back his mobile and said sympathetically,

'That kind of tactic might well have unintended consequences, possibly even contrary to those intended.'

Sashok just shrugged his shoulders. What else could he do?

In the meantime the stretched limo had made its way through the traffic jam near Waterloo and was approaching the Elephant and Castle.

'Mr Tutov,' His Lordship said, breaking the silence, 'tell me everything that's happened, right from the beginning.'

Sashok hesitated for a second. Should he trust this strange man? And how much should he tell him?

'Well,' he said finally, 'there's not much to tell. You know what this looks like? It's not even a thriller; it's some kind of travesty of one. No vast sums of money involved, no drugs and no secret documents. What do they want from me? I've no idea. First they swapped my briefcase and dumped a load of rubbish on me: a rusty alarm-clock, a dictionary, a length of greasy string.... Can you make sense of all this? And then there are the names: Byenik, Dynkin, Lyosha.... Dynkin, by the way, turns out to be a black man but he speaks like a pure con from Russian provinces.'

'Not so fast, Mr Tutov, not so fast!' the fine gentleman interrupted Sashok, 'Did you say 'Byenik'? Tell me a bit more about him.'

'What is there to say? He's a petty criminal with a tendency to behave like a clown!'

'No, no.... Give me as full a physical description of him as you can and what he sounds like. For example, has this Byenik got any gold teeth?'

'Yes, yes, he has!'

'One or two?'

'Two, I think.'

'Does he walk with a limp?

'Yes, but tries to conceal it. But I did notice.... One day I was on a train with him....'

'Oh, I see, you even travel with him. How close are you?'

'Not at all.... You don't understand....'

Sashok went bright red, lost his self-control and began arguing heatedly. And then it dawned on him: the more accurate his story, the more absurd it sounded. 'It would be great to spin them a yarn and say that Byenik was threatening me with a gun, and Dynkin had a knife to my throat and there was some sort of suspicious powder in the briefcase! Then everything would sound plausible and they might even shake my hand warmly and thank me like a hero. But when I am telling the truth, they only get sceptical. Just see how suspiciously he's looking at me, this blooming aristocrat. He probably thinks I'm a lying idiot. I wouldn't believe such rubbish, myself, if I were him either.'

The patrician forced Sashok to run through his story several times, while he turned occasionally to the computer screen and moved his hands rapidly over the key-board. It appeared he was mainly interested in Byenik. 'They're either from MI5 counter-espionage or they work for Dynkin,' reflected Sashok. And then he couldn't bear it any longer and interrupted his captor decisively,

'And where exactly are you from, Sir?'

'We?' the latter said, surprised at the question. 'We are, let's say, from Mozambique. Relatively speaking.'

Then the car, which had driven deep into Camberwell, suddenly came to a halt in a quiet alley.

'Mister Tutov,' said His Highness politely but at the same time allowing no contradiction, 'here you are going to have to get out of the car for a short while.'

Sashok was terrified.

'What for?'

'I'm sure you'd appreciate a breath of fresh air as I have the impression you're feeling a little travel sick.'

'No, I'm not!'

'Dear me, you are stubborn. We are asking you nicely; please get out of the car for a second.'

One of the hulks opened the door and gently gave Sashok a little nudge. He had no choice but to obey. 'Are they going to shoot me, or would they just drive away and leave me in the middle of the road?' he wondered. But the reality was entirely different. The doors slammed shut and Sashok stood next to the fantastic car for a minute or two under the astonished gaze of the local inhabitants, most of whom were black. 'Ah, that's it,' he thought, 'they just want to have a word with each other and didn't want me to overhear,' guessed Sashok. This time he was right. The car doors swung open again and the hulk jumped out signaling to Sashok to get back in. Then, when Sashok was settling down, he thought he saw his captor quickly hide his wonderful mobile phone under the computer. He had obviously been speaking to someone.

'Well, then, have you had a breather? Excellent! Now we can be on our way,' he said, making it sound as if Sashok had been responsible for the delay. 'There's just one thing we have to do, then we'll give you a lift home.'

The limousine stopped again.

'Please accept my apologies,' said His Magnificence, 'but we have a favour to ask you. And it might seem a little strange.'

He made a sign to the hulks who began to stretch a weird-looking thing over Sashok. He was struck dumb with amazement and indignation. In the dim light he could not quite make out what it was they were dressing him in. And only when they dragged him out of the car again did he realise that he was decked out in an ornate

Uzbek gown embroidered in gold and silk. One of the hulks came up behind him and placed an Uzbek skull-cap on his head, muttering as he did so: 'Sorry, we forgot.'

The car was standing in front of a multi-storey modern building on a so-called 'estate' – an unenviable place to live and a hot-bed of drug-taking, crime and misery. After a little while the car window was lowered and the head of one of the hulks appeared and muttered through his teeth, 'Turn a little to the right, please.' Sashok obeyed without question. He felt that he didn't care anymore. Let them have a good look at him, let them see him in all his glory, whoever 'they' were supposed to be.

Eventually the door opened again, Sashok sank onto the back seat and the car shot off. The Uzbek gown was removed and then His Lordship opened a little on-board bar, and poured two good-sized slugs of whisky, one for Sashok and one for himself.

'I don't really....' started Sashok.

'It's Laphroaig, twenty years old!' his upper-class host exclaimed indignantly.

Sashok humbly took hold of the chubby glass with the brown liquid in the bottom. He raised it to his lips. For some reason the whisky smelled of burnt wood. The thought flashed across his mind that they might have spiked it with something nasty. But he no longer cared that much.

It wasn't that Sashok liked the taste but there was no doubt that the drink somehow reconciled him a bit with reality. He could even suddenly appreciate the car, and how beautifully and silently the monster moved.

Meanwhile, His Eminence launched into a lecture on the virtues of single-malt whiskey.

Sashok had obviously dozed off because the car suddenly seemed to stop outside his house.

'You smell of spirits!' Anna-Maria said by way of a greeting.

'I'll explain everything to you ....'

'And what kind of car was that you came home in?'

'You're not going to believe it....'

'Oh, yes, I may find it hard to believe anything you say now!' Anna-Maria interrupted him. 'After our conversation I dialled 1471 and got the number you phoned from. I phoned back as I wanted to tell you what I'd left you for dinner. A nice female voice answered and told me that it was Waterloo station information service. You miserable cheat!'

It was pointless to start explaining. His wife was not in a good mood and had no desire to talk to him, so he took himself off to bed without telling her anything.

CHAPTER NINE

An incredible occurrence on the platform

So that was how it happened that Sashok never got round to telling his wife about the dodgy job on the side he was to do for Byenik. But what was he supposed to do? He had to pay off the debt and the sooner the better. At the very least and in very short order he had to get the criminal clown off his back, to forget him like a bad dream together with his even more dangerous competitors, the black-skinned gangster Dynkin and his sidekick Lyosha. And why, come to think of it, did he think of the job on the side as 'dodgy?' Well yes, of course, anything associated with Byenik was dodgy, by definition. Yet working as a guide is regarded as very respectable and acceptable among Russian newcomers to England. Just you try to get work like that! It was clean, intellectual and undemeaning work. Pretty cushy. Not at all like slaving for Mr Singh with his endless panic stations, all hands to the pumps, his rude writers, his impenetrable articles which had to be turned into masterpieces and all against surreal deadlines.

The thing that was really bad of course was that Anna-Maria knew nothing about it and was quite capable of misconstruing the situation, especially after the stupid confusion.

It was small wonder that Anna-Maria was angry. Anyone would feel annoyed in her place! Just suppose that your husband, who has never before been known to be involved in anything like this, suddenly rings you, supposedly from the office, and says that he has been held up, then spins some cock-and-bull story about his elderly boss's no longer young wife giving birth to twins and so on and so forth. All in all, you would get the feeling that he'd either lost his senses or was drunk. Add to this the fact that there were strange noises in the background sounding as if they came from a railway station, and then you find out that the call was indeed coming from a railway station (the wonders of modern technology!). And on top of all this your beloved arrives home, not by train, as he usually does, but in an unbelievably long VIP limousine, with the smell of expensive whisky on his breath. And after all this he greets you with the opening lines : 'Darling, I will explain everything....'

The next morning, without saying a word to his wife, Sashok set off for Folkestone Central to seek out the unknown 'New Russian' lady for whom he was to provide individual tourist services.

What would the woman look like? Sashok wondered. He had not had the chance to ask Byenik. He could only assume she would somehow stand out from the crowd of commuters hurrying to work. And where, exactly, was Sashok to take her? If it was a question of the usual itinerary: the Tower of London, Westminster, Piccadilly plus the obligatory shopping on Oxford Street, then there was no problem. But if the lady turned out to be a bit on the demanding side, then he could include perhaps a trip to Harrods. But what if she had some special requirements? For example, what if she really insists on seeing the best pubs in the county of Kent? Or on visiting the medieval monasteries of Southern England? Then he would have to improvise!

This is how Sashok imagined the lady: aged somewhere between forty and fifty, dressed in a provocative mink coat and with a couple of pounds of cosmetics on her face – that goes without saying. And there's no way she could be slim! She was probably the wife of some provincial boss with a cushy job in local government. Or – with Byenik you can't rule out anything! – possibly even the girlfriend of some ambitious gangster (in which case she could be quite slender after all). But anyway, whether she was slim or not, what business was it of Sashok's? He would do his day's work and then say good bye to the 'new Russian' lady and send her on her way back to Kemerovo.

All this was running through Sashok's mind as he watched the tired lady passengers standing on the platform. He was attracting some sideways glances as in England it is considered bad manners to stare at other people, particularly of the opposite sex. But it was all in vain; none of the people present resembled the target in any way, shape or form. Over there was 'Miss 7.07' – the winner of the beauty contest of all those who were waiting for this train ---the golden blond in the white coat. Sashok, who made up the judging panel all by himself, declared her victorious unanimously as there were no other serious competitors. Despite the obvious defects in her figure and somewhat chubby legs no one else was short-listed. No way could he have voted for that old girl in the shapeless hat, nor for the school-girl nymphets in their dirty trainers with cigarettes inelegantly clasped between their underage fingers. Certainly not the bespectacled school-ma'am, age indeterminate, with the absurd-looking young person's rucksack on her back (although deep down inside he felt that she must be a good, kind woman.....but her legs....no way!) Now if Anna-Maria were to appear here she would put all the rest in the shade and win hands down! Not only did she have amazingly long shapely legs, expressive brown eyes and divinely formed cheek-bones (and to be honest, Sashok had a bit of a thing about cheek-bones), and velvet skin....

Sashok suddenly remembered that when he first met Anna-Maria he was struck by her complete lack of coquettishness. She even behaved as if she did not think of herself as being attractive. This seemed a little bit odd to Sashok as he had never come across it before and, truth to tell, it took away something of the exhilaration he felt whenever he and Anna-Maria had appeared in public together in Moscow.

When Sashok first brought Anna-Maria to a party at Gavrilov's it caused a sensation. Everyone stared at her with eyes like dinner-plates: an Englishwoman who was both natural and a beauty. She turned up at a time when it was no longer dangerous to become romantically involved with a foreigner but positively advantageous. The only problem was where to find one. But Sasha had managed it!

Gavrilov took him to one side and said 'Come on, tell us, have you already … ?'

'Don't you dare ask questions like that,' Sashok said sternly.

To tell the truth, he and Anna-Maria hardly knew each other at that time. Gavrilov himself had introduced them without even realising it. The day before, serious events had taken place in Moscow around the White House, Boris Yeltsin's headquarters where people had gathered trying to resist the Communist putsch. There were even barricades being erected there. Sashok had found himself stuck in Moscow and Gavrilov had dragged him along to the White House (they were both on vacation), letting slip the puzzling phrase 'it might turn out useful.' Sashok had no idea in what way it could be beneficial to them but then the ways of Gavrilov were always a mystery. So, when he shot off somewhere to go to a party Sashok remained alone. He walked around an overturned trolleybus and then (purely out of politeness) helped some sullen bearded guys drag heavy bits of rusty scrap iron onto the barricades. And suddenly he saw a beautiful young woman, obviously dressed like a foreigner and obviously behaving like a foreigner. She was attempting, without any visible signs of success, to have a conversation with a mad-looking soldier who was leaning out of a tank.

'She's either French or Dutch and, obviously, speaks English,' thought Sashok and decided to her aid. But as soon as she opened her mouth there was no doubt that this beauty came from the country which was Sashok's speciality.

'Perhaps Prokofiev was right after all,' thought Sashok, admiring Anna-Maria, 'English women really are beautiful: just for some reason I had not seen any like this before.'

He tried his very best, demonstrating his interpreter's talents. He felt inspired. The man in the tank answered in monosyllables and Sashok was forced to be inventive in order to show off his knowledge of subtle idioms, intellectually challenging grammatical constructions and complicated *consecutio temporum,* agreement of tenses. Against his will and purely for the sake of linguistic bravado Sashok transformed Pavel, the soldier in the tank, into a passionate and fearless protector of Russian democracy who was prepared to risk arrest and even death in the name of freedom. But what Pavel really said, scratching his head, was 'Let the battalion commander sort it out with the political officer; they are smart and clever, they went to the Academy, it's their call, not mine, I am a soldier, I don't have to think!'

Sashok didn't fully register it himself, but at some point he too, started to sound like a fearless revolutionary. In fact, Anna-Maria took it for granted, because, as it became clear later, she did observe Sashok selflessly dragging the scrap iron up onto the barricade. In the end, he couldn't bring himself to disappoint her and admit his lack of interest in politics. At some point Sashok noticed that this pretty English girl had begun to cast admiring glances his way and not at hard-bitten Pavel in his dusty helmet. But still he didn't expect her to be so quick to accept his invitation 'to go and celebrate the victory of democracy' that evening. But she did!

One of the dearest memories for Sashok was the moment, some time towards the end of Gavrilov's party, when a crowd of University friends turned up and Gavrilov introduced Anna-Maria to them in English: 'This is Sasha's girlfriend.' She burst out laughing but – amazingly! - made no attempt to contradict him. The suggestion took Sashok's breath away.... This beautiful English woman with stunning teeth, legs and cheek-bones and eyes like Julia Roberts', this natural English woman, for Heaven's sake, could be Sashok's girlfriend! He felt as though everyone present was staring at him struck dumb with a mixture of envy and admiration; there he was, an absolutely ordinary kind of guy, nothing special, how had he managed to pull off such a trick? Admittedly, he was by no means ugly and had done rather well at university, particularly in English. He had been also moderately successful dating Lyenka from another stream but now, suddenly, without rhyme or reason, he found himself in a totally different class of mortals.

Of course, thought Sashok, all this was in the naïve year of 1991. And none of those who had gathered at Gavrilov's place that evening had any idea about the town of Folkestone where Anna-Maria lived with her parents or about the platform with grass coming up through the asphalt and on which fat, strutting cheeky seagulls wandered as if they were waiting for a train. They (not the seagulls but the Moscow students of '91) had not the slightest idea what a mortgage was, they knew absolutely nothing about deposits and interest rates. They couldn't have guessed how dreary those matters could be, what a millstone round your neck. Nor did they understand what it was to wait for a late museum-piece of a train with steel doors, which slammed shut with a deafening racket, right next to every bank of seats. And the train would then dawdle with all the speed of a tortoise for the next hour-and-a-half or two hours (if you were lucky) to its destination in London.

On this occasion, it is true, the 7.07 was only three minutes late. 'She's missed it, the wretched woman,' thought Sashok gloomily of his New Russian client. 'Or, maybe, the clown has tricked me again and I am wasting my time.'

But then ... then there was Anna-Maria on the platform! This was precisely what he feared might happen. By sod's law, by incredible coincidence his wife, who very seldom travelled up to London at that time in the morning, suddenly came to the station at the very moment when he was supposed to meet his client. It was just the sort of thing Anna-Maria would do: to come running up to see him off and give him a tender good-bye kiss as a sign of reconciliation. Oh God! What if she were to see him now with some female Russian pleb!

Sashok's first reaction was to hide. But where? The gents' toilet was closed again 'due to vandalism' (British vandals, for some reason, nurture a particular dislike of gents' toilets). But what if Anna-Maria had already spotted him? A game of hide-and-seek would only make matters worse. He had one hope: that the blasted 'new Russian woman' would indeed turn out to be a myth. Or, at least, would be late. Sashok looked around one more time and....hurrah! There was nobody who even remotely resembled a woman from Siberia. Not only that but the train doors were already slamming shut and the travellers were by now settling themselves down in the antiquated carriages. It was the usual people who travelled on the 7.07 to Charing Cross. 'Perhaps I'm in luck for once in my life,' thought Sashok.

Anna-Maria frequently laughed at Sashok's lack of attentiveness: she always said that he never noticed how his wife was dressed. But this time he could not possibly have failed to notice what strange clothes she was wearing. She had squeezed herself into a figure-hugging black jump-suit, almost a leotard. On her head she wore a black head-scarf and on her feet- could it be trainers? And she was carrying a black hand-bag. 'A real ninja…. The only thing missing is a black face-covering,' ran through Sashok's mind. 'Why all this dressing-up?'

But then he saw something even more striking: Anna-Maria walked past him, just eighteen inches away, and pretended not to notice him. She opened the carriage door. And only then did she turn to face Sashok and made a commanding gesture with her head which said: 'follow me!' Stunned and speechless Sashok meekly climbed into the carriage. They sat down opposite each other and the train moved off.

'Where's the toilet? I have to get changed,' Anna-Maria said in an unusually deep, hoarse voice.

Sashok, who had still not regained his senses, did not say a word and simply pointed to the arrow above the window. Anna-Maria nodded and set off in the direction indicated. Two seconds later she had completely disappeared from his view. And only then did he grasp the significance of the incredible phenomenon he had just witnessed: Anna-Maria had spoken in Russian! And without any trace of an accent. Sashok felt the goose-pimples running all over his skin.

CHAPTER TEN

A mysterious double

What a to-do! Obviously, there was no way ever that this could be Anna-Maria. How on earth did he manage to confuse his own wife with a stranger? But there was no denying that the resemblance was astonishing.

When 'Anna-Maria' returned from the toilet she had changed into an elegant light beige jacket and trousers. She sat down opposite Sashok as if absolutely nothing extraordinary had happened and began nonchalantly powdering her nose. Sashok started to look her up and down, timidly at first but then more and more openly as it became obvious that his behaviour was causing no embarrassment to his travelling companion; she even smiled encouragingly when she noticed his tense look. Sashok could not take his eyes off her and thought: *How could the Good Lord or Nature or whatever, have created a being so closely resembling another one?* The first idea that entered his head was that Anna-Maria had a long-lost twin sister. But no; on closer examination some small but important distinguishing features were noticeable. First of all, their ears were different: not for nothing do people say that immigration officers and border guards first of all compare a person's ears with those on their passport photograph. This lady's ears were noticeably larger and less elegant than Anna-Maria's. But for the rest.....her hair, quite extraordinary, was exactly the same colour, but just a tiny bit thicker than his wife's. But her hair style was the same - loose curls down to the shoulders. And another thing: there was no birth-mark on the right side of her neck. The eyes were nearly the same but there was an almost imperceptible difference; this girl's were just that little bit bigger, and her pupils were perhaps a bit darker. On the other hand the girl's make-up (Anna-Maria hardly ever used it) did make quite a difference. But the eyes.... The main difference was a kind of unfamiliar expression in the eyes, an unaccustomed steely flash which you could never see in Anna-Maria's. Or was Sashok imagining it?

Suddenly it came to him: this woman was a retouched portrait of Anna-Maria! And the nose - the nose was a fraction, just a few millimetres shorter than the original. The lips were slightly fuller (it has to be said if Anna-Maria had any physical imperfection, it was that her lips were a bit on a thin side). And, maybe, this lady's cheek-bones were slightly more refined, although there was nothing wrong with Anna-Maria's. In sum, in other words, if you ignore the ears this was a copy improved by a few per cent.

Meanwhile the object under scrutiny had completed cosmetic manipulations and then she, in her turn, began to study Sashok.

'Well then, say something,' she said suddenly, 'we not going to travel all the way up to London in silence?'

It took a while for Sashok to pull himself together but then he said the first thing that came into his head,

'That outfit you're wearing ... it suits you really well.'

'I should hope so! It cost me an arm and a leg! You don't want to know how much. But then it's not every day I come to Europe.'

They fell silent. Then Sashok, hesitantly, said:

'Tell me, was it Byenik who sent you?'

'Who?' said the unknown lady with such a cheerful childish giggle that, for all the steel and all the make-up, she looked like a naughty little girl.

'Byenik,' said Sashok, confused.

'Oh, yes, well of course it was him, Enik-Byenik.... How could I forget?'

She tried to put on a serious face for a moment but could not restrain herself and began giggling again in such an infectious manner that Sashok joined in the laughter, which quite surprised him.

'But....' he said, finding it difficult to talk and laugh at the same time, 'You are ... you're ... the same lady whom....

'Whom, whom....' she repeated.

'Whom I was supposed to accompany on a journey through Britain,' said Sashok, managing with difficulty to finish off what he was saying.

The stranger suddenly stopped short and said in a stern, business-like tone of voice,

'And you are Alexander, also known as Sasha, my guide for a few days, unless I'm mistaken. By the way, my name is Anastasia, but you can call me Nastya when there are no Englishmen around to hear you.'

'Oh, so you've already been warned....'

'Yes there was one guy who made fun of me: *are you really nasty or just naughty?* Apparently 'nasty' means 'horrible' and 'naughty' means 'mischievous.' Am I right?'

'Well, something like that, but in this context 'naughty' can also hint at something bad.'

'My English isn't good enough to appreciate hints: 'Please', 'thank you', 'cool', 'special price', 'face control'... that is all I know.'

And Nastya laughed so delightfully again that Sashok could not help joining in. The thought flashed through his mind: 'why can't Anna-Maria enjoy herself like that?'

Within a few minutes they were chatting like friends. Sashok had not been in such good form for ages and it was a long time since anyone had listened to him so attentively, or expressed such genuine surprise at the absurdities of English life or laughed so heartily at his jokes.

For instance, he said that the English were a strange lot and like nobody else. It was quite impossible for anyone to fully understand them but he, Sashok, tried to figure them out intuitively. Sometimes it worked, sometimes it didn't. And examples of this strangeness? When you're dealing with them, the main thing is the art of understatement. Apart from the weather you must not speak too favourably about anyone or anything. And you can't be too critical either, though, once again, the weather is an exception. You can swear about it if you want, use very bad language. But to the question 'How are you?' you must always, in almost all situations, reply 'I'm fine'. Unless of course you're in the final stages of cancer, or you've got blood pouring out of open wounds, or your wife has fallen under a train, then, ok, you can say something along the lines of 'not too well.' But remember that being this open presupposes that you are close to the other person or have known them for a long time. And you mustn't boast or talk about your own achievements or if you do, you should hint at it or do it in passing as if it's something very unimportant. And it's quite ok too to make fun of your own country though they won't take it from foreigners.

If you get out into the middle of a street and burst out sobbing or laughing or tear your hair out, then it is considered good form for others not to notice. True, if there are grounds for thinking you need an ambulance, then someone may well come up to you quickly and ask, 'Are you all right?' But if you let people know that you are OK, they are all confused and apologize and rush away, even if it's obvious that you are at death's door. This is because the biggest sin you can commit is to interfere in other people's business and to breach their privacy.

'So they're cold fish, they've no souls,' concluded Nastya.

'Oh no, you can't say that! It's just that everything is hidden away deep down. And down there inside them, it appears, complex and subtle processes are at work. If all of a sudden you ask for help the typical Englishman may drop everything he's doing, go and show you the way, he may even get a map out of his car and open it up for you. If he finds a lost purse or a mobile phone chances are he will look after it for you. They insist on saving the pennies to a ridiculous degree but, even if they are on a tight budget, they'll give to charity at every opportunity. On more than one occasion people have offered me help - sometimes a loan, sometimes real giving. And I have Russian friends whose daughter's schooling was paid for by a gentleman who was not at all rich and who hardly knew them. And he went on doing it until they found their feet. It's all the same to me, he said, I always give a thousand pounds a year to charity anyway.

'He sounds touched in the head,' muttered Nastya

'Not a bit of it. It's just the way they are….a bit eccentric. But that's the British middle class for you. Society as a whole here has become much polarised. For centuries talent was sucked out of the lower classes with the help of the grammar schools, and what was left in the residue, God only knows. Judging by some of the signs the football hooligan classes are not just people from a different country: they are from a different planet. And then there are a huge number of foreigners, all with their different customs, who have flooded into the country. And that includes our good Russian selves who couldn't care less about these English niceties.'

'Maybe in time we could turn them into normal people?' Nastya suggested. 'But the way they dress…….it's just bizarre.'

'Yes,' Sashok agreed, 'among educated or middle class people it's considered rather vulgar to dress well or to care about your appearance. Obviously you mustn't look like a tramp or a trollop but clothes which are old, worn, darned, that's just the thing. They don't know much about standing in queues and that's why they put up with them stoically on the rare occasions when they have to. Say when an aeroplane or a bus or a train has broken down or is late or cancelled. In Russia people would have been shouting long ago, swearing, letting their feelings out and threatening to punch someone in the face. But not here. Here they'll stand meekly for hours, not saying a word, or talking among themselves quietly and politely ….it's completely daft! They usually allow local services and public transport to make complete fools of them. They take it without a murmur. Why? Maybe because they are really all individualists to the core. They can't behave like a crowd. But sometimes you have to. On commuter trains, on the underground, their behaviour's absurd, they're like sheep. Byenik was right about that. They cluster round the doors and they'll never think to pass down inside where there's plenty of space, not until someone with a continental mindset raises his voice and says 'Will you move down a bit?' or just 'Move down.' In English it sounds very rude if you don't add 'please' or 'will you.' If you translate this into Russian you'd have to say something like 'Move flicking down, you blockheads!' Then they will move, though a bit unwillingly. People don't usually give up their seats in public transport except to pregnant women and invalids. Or, for instance, just think about a situation like this: a man on a train gets up and goes to the toilet, leaving his newspaper and jacket on his seat. When he comes back he sees that his jacket has been stuffed onto the overhead rack and there's somebody else, an old fellow sitting in his seat and reading his newspaper. The old fellow realizes straight away that the owner of the paper and jacket has come back; he apologises, jumps up and invites him to take his rightful place. But it doesn't feel right to make an elderly gentleman stand, so the hapless passenger has to stand for the rest of the journey. But you haven't heard the crucial bit of the story yet: the lady sitting in the next seat turns bright red. She is clearly very embarrassed. After a good deal of hesitation she plucks up courage and explains that the old man did ask if the seat was taken. But she did not commit herself to a definite answer. 'You know, it's one of those awkward situations,' she says. 'How do you mean? What's so awkward about it? Why didn't you announce to the whole train, as people in Russia would have done: 'Yes, there was someone sitting here. He's probably gone to the loo.' That is what I wanted to tell that lady but didn't. Was too embarrassed to say what I thought.'

'A-ha! So you've gone native!' Nastya said with a grin.

'Not really.... But one can't avoid local influences entirely....'

'Well, well, well.... OK, now tell me more about those British eccentrics.'

'Frankly, their Eccentricity does sometimes border on insanity. A few days ago there was a family on a train, mum, dad and two small kids about eight to ten. He's a model father and all the way he's telling his children amusing and instructive tales and setting riddles and puzzles. Every now and then he jumps up from his seat and runs off to the buffet or the toilet – but in his socks, no shoes. Eccentric - but not excessively so. Nobody pays any attention to him. Here you can come across people carrying suitcases on their heads, their hair in impossible plaits; wearing a jacket and tie above the waist and shorts or heaven knows what below. (The only thing considered taboo is wearing socks with open sandals – that's a complete no-no.) But then the family arrives at their destination, Tonbridge. All four of them get out onto the platform and for some reason wave the departing train off. The father is bare foot even though it's cold out, it's November. They smile gleefully, wave their hands in farewell and shout something in chorus. I tried to nake out what exactly they were shouting, and you know what it was? 'Bye-bye, shoes!'. The shoes which the head of the family had taken a dislike to had been wrapped up carefully in a newspaper and then in a plastic bag, and then placed on the overhead rack. 'Good bye, shoes! Bon voyage!'

Nastya laughed and then asked,

'Tell me, what's it like to live with an Englishwoman?'

'Well, it's OK. Almost. It's annoying that the English don't wash dishes like normal people do - they just splosh them about a bit in soapy water. And they wear their outdoor shoes in the house. And you've got to put the toilet seat down after using it. If you forget, you'll be committing an unforgivable sin.'

'And do they still have separate taps for hot and cold water?'

'Of course they do…. But there's something else lacking, which is much more difficult to get used to.'

'What's that?'

'The fact that you've always got to keep your distance, you're not meant to look into each other's souls. For a Russian this can be very hard,' said Sashok.

He then fell into a shocked silence: why ever all of a sudden had he opened up his innermost thoughts to a stranger, to a woman whom he did not even know? She was so like Anna-Maria and at the same time so different maybe that is why he was telling her things which he could never bring himself to say to his lawfully-wedded wife.

Suddenly Anastasia yawned and Sashok noticed a hint of a glaze in her eyes.

'You must be tired,' he said, 'how have you been travelling: by train or by ferry?'

Nastya gave a little snort in reply. She hid her eyes. Then she snorted again. Finally she could contain herself no longer and burst out laughing.

'Nonsense. I'm wide awake. Can you really not guess how I got to England?'

Sashok looked at Nastya and remembered how she was dressed in black when he first saw her, and the most improbable conjectures came into his head.

CHAPTER ELEVEN

Sashok's head spins

Sashok was stunned. It was as obvious as the nose on your face that there, sitting in front of him on the train, was a real live illegal immigrant who had been smuggled into the United Kingdom by some secret means. What was it they used to say in the days of the old Soviet Union? She had 'violated the state border'. That's the expression!

In addition, this beautiful woman (who, as if by magic, resembled his wife) hinted at the unbelievable manner in which she had crossed the border. It was a terrifying thought but it appeared that this woman had gained entry into Britain by way of the tunnel under the English Channel. Perhaps she had even walked all the way!

The town of Folkestone, incidentally, is famous throughout the world because it is situated just by the tunnel entrance. On several occasions Sashok had read about desperate Afghans and Iraqis who had attempted to enter the country this way. One day they had also caught a Russian on the British side who told the journalists that it took him five hours to walk through the tunnel and that he had successfully dodged the trains and kept his strength up by eating grapes as these quenched his thirst at the same time as providing his body with sugar.

Sashok stared at Anastasia and was amazed at how unruffled she appeared after her adventures, how remarkably fresh she looked. Her velvet eyes gleamed. It was difficult to believe that she had just completed an exhausting and dangerous journey entailing sleepless nights. Then it crossed Sashok's mind: perhaps he should not believe her. Would it not be more logical to suppose that all this was just another one of Byenik's little games? First, he had landed Sashok with a briefcase which looked exactly like his own but belonged to somebody else. And now he was talking to a woman who looked like his own wife's identical twin but was actually somebody else. These tricks were designed to fool him, but now he'd had enough!

'Would you like some grapes?' Anastasia said, interrupting his train of thought.

'Grapes!?' Sashok yelled so loud that Anastasia pulled back the cellophane bag containing a bunch of deep-red, juicy grapes.

'What's the matter? What is it? Doesn't your religion allow you to eat grapes?'

'What's religion got to do with it?' Now it was Sashok's turn to be surprised.

'Well, I don't know. Some people aren't allowed to eat pork, others can't eat beef and then others are forbidden to eat fish without scales. Perhaps your church forbids grapes.... How should I know? You shouted out so loud....'

'No, it's just that I didn't expect…. It is grapes that…..'

'Grapes - what?'

'Never mind…. It's nothing. I just…. It's not important, it's nonsense, let's forget it.' said Sashok, embarrassed. 'I am, in fact, Orthodox Russian, but I don't go to church.'

'That's a mistake.'

'Why is it a mistake?'

'Because you should, just in case……'

'In case what?'

'Don't pretend you don't understand!'

Nastya seemed to be getting a little angry and her inner steel came to the surface and shone in her eyes. It also sharpened the features of her face so that her resemblance to Anna-Maria evaporated: now in front of Sashok sat a totally different woman. 'Better not argue with this one,' his inner voice advised him. 'Oh, how wise you are!' Sashok retorted and then said out loud,

'Englishmen, and I mean the genuine natives of England, never discuss subjects such as the existence of God with people whom they do not know well.'

'But you're not an Englishman, are you?'

'Of course I'm not. You can't become an Englishman. You have to be born here and grow up in a proper English family and absorb something special from childhood.'

'What exactly?' Anastasia was clearly beginning to take an interest in the conversation and once again assumed a startling resemblance to Anna-Maria.

'Do you know what they say? You can't be a real Englishman unless you can pronounce the word 'really' with seventeen different intonations.

'Really?' Anastasia said in English and again laughed infectiously.

Sashok laughed too.

'And you....'

'What about me?'

'You've found the eighteenth way!'

Anastasia laughed happily and said:

'Tell me honestly, do you really like all this nonsense?'

'Do you know, I sometimes feel there's something to all this stoicism and sense of fair play. Something attractive about it, even if it does drive you mad on occasions. Sometimes you think this is just arrogance by another name ... but you know what they say about the difference between the English and the French? They both think they're superior to everybody else. But if the French look down on the rest of humanity then the English just pity us, they see us as poor souls who did not have the good fortune to be born English.'

'Well, there's no need to pity me,' said Nastya forcefully.

'I can easily see that ,' Sashok agreed politely.

They said nothing for a short while. Anastasia looked out of the window, obviously mulling over what she had just heard. Then she asked,

'But these Englishmen of yours, if they are such stoics, why do they run around like animals on the Greek and Spanish islands? I've read about them and I've seen on the telly how they get smashed out of their minds and run about naked.'

'They need to let their hair down now and again. Here in Great Britain they have to control themselves and pretend that they are set apart from the rest of humanity; but once they're abroad it's as if none of this matters.'

'Sounds like hypocrisy to me,' Anastasia snorted. Sashok wanted to contradict her, but just at that moment they both noticed a man sitting further down the carriage who was nodding his head at them vigorously. He was trying his best to attract their attention, smiling, winking and giving them the thumbs-up sign. Now, when he was sure that he had caught Sashok's eye, he displayed his obvious delight, waving his hands about and shouting.

'You all right, mate?' he yelled.

'Who's that nutter?' Anastasia asked, alarmed.

'That's Harry.'

'A friend of yours?'

'No, he lives in the same town but I don't know where exactly. He's got wonderful children, a boy and a girl. I think he's a burglar.'

'What?'

'A burglar. He empties houses but officially he's unemployed.'

'How did you find out he's a burglar?'

'Word gets around..........It's a small town. Everyone knows everybody's business. He gets arrested, police search his place but can never prove anything. He's very smart. My in-laws reckon he's done us over four times.'

'Are you serious? Is that the way people behave here? And now he's nodding his head and is all friendly with you? Looks like he's a family friend!'

'But he probably thinks he is. He's been attached to us for so many years.'

'Sounds crazy to me. Can't somebody lie in wait for him and smash his head in?'

'Oh no; it's better not to get involved in that sort of thing. The judges here are pretty hard on people who overstep the mark when it comes to self-defence and they hand out hefty punishments.'

'Even if the criminals are caught red-handed?'

'This is not America. Burglars caught for the first time here are not usually sent to prison; they're just fined or given a suspended sentence. But if you inflict serious injury on them or accidentally kill them, then you'll do porridge. They could even send you down for life.'

'You're pulling my leg!'

'No I'm not! I myself find it hard to believe even now. My mother-in-law explained to me that the thinking is that you can't equate property with a life or somebody's health. And also, the overwhelming majority of people have their furniture, electrical goods and even their clothes and the food in the fridge insured. That's how my in-laws have replaced everything four times. It's a lot of hassle, of course. Harry likes to talk about the advantages of insurance. If he comes and joins us now I guarantee he'll try to sell us a policy or two. He's a real pain in the neck.'

'All your Englishmen, generally speaking then, are nut-cases and masochists,' she said, 'and I've heard that they enjoy a good whipping.'

'Well, yes, I've read about that, too. The French laugh at them and talk about the 'English vice.' The English probably have taken this thing further than anyone else.'

'What thing?'

'The exploration of the thin line between pain and pleasure.'

That's when something happened to Anastasia. Suddenly, there was the hint of a glaze in her eyes and a fleeting shudder passed over her face. Staring at Sashok, she began licking her lips. Sashok detected (or was he just imagining it?) some kind of signal or impulse which made him feel distinctly uneasy.

'Perhaps you'd like to have lunch?' he asked in an attempt to hide his embarrassment.

'Good idea,' said Anastasia, averting his eyes. 'Let's get off as soon as possible; I've had enough travelling.'

'There's a nice little place near here, a lovely pub with a view over the river.'

'But can we get something to eat in this…. How do you call it? A pub?'

'Easy! It is true, though, that they're not all open at this time. But this one is and it's not very far from here, near the vegetable market. It opens at five o'clock in the morning.'

Meanwhile the weather had cleared up. The sky was blue and the sun was shining and in its rays Anastasia gleamed. Walking alongside her Sashok was overcome with strange feelings. Despite the awful Mr Byenik, despite the depressing feeling that he, Sashok, was once again the target of some idiotic practical joke or foul scheming designed with certain malice aforethought, he was overcome with the desire to take this beautiful woman by the arm and perhaps even lay a kiss on her peach-like skin. How easy it was for him to forget everything and allow himself to…. Simply because she bore such an unbelievable likeness to his lawful wedded wife! But for all that she was a tad more common, just a touch more sensual than Anna-Maria. In fact, she was a bit vulgar. But this did not make her any the less attractive; in truth, just the opposite.

There weren't too many people in the 'Frog and Crown' at this unearthly hour; just a few regulars hovered around the bar. Sashok ordered a 'full English' for Anastasia: fried egg, bacon, special sausages, fried tomatoes and slices of hot buttered toast. And she set about consuming the lot with great gusto.

'Would you like to try a glass of draught ale?' Sashok asked on the off chance.

'Oh, I've got to try this wonder. What's it like, actually? Something like beer?'

'Not really. It's brewed in a different way, not unlike our fermented *kvass*. It's served warm, not chilled.'

'Is it strong?'

'Reasonably.'

'Then I'd better wait till later.'
'Would you like a shandy, then?'
'What's that?'
'It's a mixture of beer or ale with lemonade.'
'What? You must be joking!'
'No, I'm not. It's no joke.... It's another national drink, not so strong and intended for the ladies.'
'Well, I'm not one of those ladies.'
'I already guessed that.'
'And who on earth thought of mixing sweet lemonade with beer!?'

It took Anastasia a while to regain her composure. When she did finally manage it she said quietly,

'Sasha, I need to book into a hotel......not an expensive one but one of those, y'know, where they don't pay an awful lot of attention to you. But at the same time it has to be near the centre.'

Turning his mind to the problem, Sashok was able to come up with a whole bunch of cheap (and some rather doubtful) hotels in the area around Victoria. They clearly matched the criteria specified by Anastasia.

She wanted to make the journey in 'a real London taxi' and was delighted with their traditional design. 'It's so authentic,' she exclaimed with satisfaction as she paid the fare.

The Cornwall Hotel (no stars) was hardly luxurious, but it was reasonably clean. A sleepy-looking Philippino behind the desk produced a registration form for them to sign.

'A double room?' he asked.'

Sashok was about to open his mouth and say 'No, certainly not. The lady's travelling alone and I'm merely keeping her company,' but he was too late. Nastya beat him to it.

'Yes, yes, we're husband and wife,' she said as she gave Sashok a painful prod in the side with her elbow and whispered:

'Fill the form in.'

'Foreign guests have to give their passport details,' muttered the Phillipino, looking to one side.

'No, no we're locals, from Folkestone,' Anastasia hurried to assure the hotel employee in her dreadful English.

'In that case you only have to give your address', he replied.

'Write your address,' Nastya whispered in Sashok's ear.

He hesitated for a few moments and then – in for a penny, in for a pound! – he filled in the form using the names Mr and Mrs Tutov. He somehow felt it was OK as Nastya and Anna-Maria were as like as two peas in a pod.

'Come on, you can help me settle in,' Nastya said quietly in a special hoarse voice which sent Sashok's head into a spin.

CHAPTER TWELVE

The sweet abyss

And so it was that Sashok cheated on his wife. He did not even understand himself how it happened. He could not work it out in time. On previous occasions he had always been able to steer away from temptation at the last moment. Well, OK, OK, perhaps he *had* been weak on one previous occasion, but it had been an unfortunate occurrence in completely bizarre circumstances. And anyway, as the Germans say, einmal ist keinmal, once is the same as never. And, bear in mind, Sashok had repented. He had repented, and vowed never to take risks again. And that, surely, was right: why should he gamble his well-being and his peace of mind – not just his own but his beloved wife's too? No, he decided, a man has to fight his natural impulses, keep them under control. All the more so as sensual pleasure was followed by strange feeling of melancholy, in fact, he was pretty miserable and depressed. You had to ask yourself: was it worth it? And you end up answering your own question: no, it wasn't.

But this time it was different. In the first place he wasn't really sad or depressed, well almost not. (In fact Anastasia had noticed something in his look and suddenly stroked his cheek and said tenderly: 'Post coitus omni animal tristi'. 'After sex all animals are sad,' Sashok translated almost absent-mindedly, and then asked 'So, sprechen Sie Latin, then?' 'No, no.' she replied, laughing. 'It just came out: it's the only expression I know.')

So, no, honestly, this time he felt no melancholy to speak of. And anyway things had got pretty confused from the very beginning. Who could have imagined what this 'new Russian woman' would look like? Being beautiful was one thing but why on top of that should she be so strangely like his wife, Anna-Maria? Quite simply they had the same face (with the bodies it was a bit more complicated, but that came out later on). Which is why all his defence mechanisms failed to engage! The mechanisms believed this was someone who was, very close, very familiar, very dear. 'Relax, everything's OK, there's no need to get uptight,' that was the signal he was getting. So Sashok relaxed, and then some. He had it clearly in mind what he would say to his wife: 'yes, I lost my head, because I fell in love with...the most beautiful woman in the world! She's so beautiful that she looks exactly like you!' And of course, Anna-Maria would be bound to understand!

But his inner voice begged to differ: 'she won't understand! No way! And don't even begin to hope she will.' Sashok was cast down for a minute, imagining the tears in Anna-Maria's beautiful eyes. ('Hey, hang on for a second, whose eyes are we talking about? Eh? Those aren't the right ones! It's a mix-up! It's Nastya's eyes you are dreaming about!' chirped his inner voice maliciously).

In a word, Sashok was completely confused. And to muster enough concentration to work it all out was beyond him. From the outside it looked as if Sashok was sitting, as usual, on the train which he always took in the evening to come home from work. But in reality he was still in that cheap and disgusting little room in 'The Cornwall Hotel' next to Victoria station.

From time to time Sashok comes up from the gloomy depths, looks in bewilderment at the world of the railway carriage around him and immediately remembers the feeling of guilt which he is supposed to be suffering from. His anguish lasts a few minutes and then he sinks back into his magical abyss. Oh, what unbelievable sensations he felt! They could not be conveyed in words, only in movements and gestures, in strange sweet melody that nobody else could hear, in something which resides under his skin, in his glands perhaps, or in his red blood corpuscles and which has no name. Sashok wiggles his fingers and remembers what they had been up to just a few hours earlier. But, it's not only a memory, oh, no, he's living it all over again! He puts his face in his hands and feels Nastya's burning lips on his skin. He squeezes his legs so tight it hurts and.... He feels, he hears and he sees. Everything that has happened in the last few hours has been stored somewhere in the pupils of his eyes. He sees visions of wild, unimaginable scenes and a sweet shiver runs through his whole body. He wants to leap up and shout meaningless words in an unknown tongue. And a couple of times, when he came up to the surface, it seemed to him that he really had been shouting something incoherent, so odd was the look on the faces of the passengers around him. But maybe he was just imagining it. In any case he had no time to sort things out with them and he sank once more with delight into his abyss.

Now it's as if he and Anastasia are squeezing again into the tiny low ground floor room in the hotel. A sturdy double bed takes up so much space that it is difficult not to look at it, but Sashok makes the effort. Now he opens his mouth to say 'OK, I'll be off now, I'll see you in the lobby.' But just at that point as Nastya was trying to get past him he momentarily felt her breast brushing against him and his vocal chords failed him. Meanwhile, Anastasia disappeared into the bathroom and Sashok was left standing there like a statue, stunned and thinking about another important difference between these two women who were so alike. Then his inner voice muttered quietly: 'Now everything depends on what she looks like when she comes out of the bathroom. You'll know then if she touched you accidentally or not.'

Sashok got the answer when Anastasia emerged from the bathroom half undressed. Or, more precisely, hardly dressed at all. And oh, yes, those breasts..... It was such a pleasure even to look at them, so stunning they were. Not just large, but also firm and impudently protruding with beautifully formed large pink nipples. Sashok never knew such breasts existed. Anna-Maria's, to be honest, were simply not in the same league..... Whew! Sashok had not managed to gather his wits before Anastasia was already cuddling up against him. Without her heels she turned out to be much shorter than he was. 'And shorter than Anna-Maria, too....' said his inner voice, trying to restore a sense of fairness. But Sashok was not interested in fairness, he was already being borne away to realms where no inner voices can be heard, and where not much else could be heard either. In Anastasia's eyes there was now a strange expression of dreamy intoxication, her lips were running over his neck, his cheek, now they were creeping up to his ear and were almost inaudibly whispering (or was Sashok imagining it?) 'Take off my panties....'

These panties turned out to be triangular in shape and a remarkable bright green colour. Anna-Maria, as Sashok now suddenly realised, wore quite different ones, ordinary and clearly old-fashioned. This little triangle was specially designed to drive a man crazy. It revealed much more than it covered. It both promised and concealed a burning secret.

Many years later Sashok would regularly wake up at night from one and the same dream in which his hand would be reaching for the green panties. There would no longer be any erotic component to the dream, just a feeling of shock and surprise. The dream would be black and white but somehow it was a known fact that the panties were green. And, as a rule, there would be no trace of Anastasia herself in the dream.

Sashok resurfaced again after yet another trip to his magical abyss when he heard someone speaking loudly in his ear and even seemed to be shaking him by the arm. Unbelievably, it was Harry again!

'So we're on the same train again, Mr Tutov, and in the same carriage!' Harry exclaimed jauntily.

Sashok wanted to say something rude but stopped himself at the last moment.

'Well it's not all that surprising. After all, we do live in the same town,' he observed in a conciliatory fashion.

'That's certainly true! All the same I've been up and down to London quite a lot recently but I haven't seen you for ages. How are your parents getting on?'

'I take it you mean my father-in-law and mother-in-law? They are both in good health.'

'And your wife?'

'My wife? What about her?' answered Sashok automatically and then choked as if a bone had got stuck in his throat.

What a good question! Indeed, how was his wife, Anna-Maria? What would he feel like when he saw her? How would he behave? What would he say to her? Those thoughts made him shudder. He was sure he would give himself away, that his voice would betray him, he would not be able to look her in the eye and his face would either turn red or white.

And with this Sashok sank back into his thoughts but this time they took on a highly alarming turn. Strange to tell, up till this moment he had not thought about what he was going to do now. Would he lose Anna-Maria? What a dreadful thought! Should he renounce Anastasia just when such delightful prospects had suddenly opened up? That would be a shame! Should he try to live a double life? Sashok did not have the stomach for that sort of thing. He would lose the plot very quickly.

Any activity, thought Sashok, requires a professional approach and marital infidelity was no exception. And, as was so often the case in life's difficult moments, he remembered his class-mate and mentor Gavrilov. That was a consummate professional, a veteran, who knew just how to cover his tracks and was very successful with young girls! But at the same time he was a remarkable family man, respected not only by his wife but by his-in-laws as well. Yet Gavrilov nearly always had a mistress or two on the side. 'Man's heart is not a stone!' Gavrilov taught Sashok.

But Sashok was no Gavrilov and his friend's guidelines were of little use to him. Nevertheless he did wonder what course of action Gavrilov would recommend in these particular circumstances. What would he say if he knew that the two women were so phenomenally alike? Sashok would have to ring him and ask his advice.

Not surprisingly, Sashok did not pay too much attention to Harry who was expatiating on the insurance market, on the relative merits of the theft policy of one company as opposed to another. At length Sashok realized that Harry was pushing for an answer to a particular question. And almost unthinkingly he blurted out 'Norwich Union,' assuming that Harry was enquiring which company Sashok's family was insured with. And a dismal thought flashed across Sashok's mind: 'he's thinking of doing us over again.'

People said of Harry that he was a burglar, but a good burglar, a man with a conscience. When he went on a job he always preferred to be sure that his intended victim had all his possessions insured. In this way he could call himself a kind of socialist working for the redistribution of wealth. After all, these insurance companies are so rich and make such fortunes out of their customers that they would not be any worse off.

'Norwich Union?' Harry repeated after Sashok. 'What have they got to do with it? No, I said that when I saw you with your wife today she looked a bit different somehow. Either she's lost a bit of weight or something....'

'Wow, what an observant fellow' thought Sashok, and then said out loud,

'No, no, everything's fine with Anna-Maria.'

'I must have imagined it then. But that's not surprising since I seldom see her. And I'd never seen you two together before. Doesn't she ever go up to London with you?'

Sashok was already beginning to find the conversation a bit suspicious and Harry, as if reading his thoughts, promptly changed the subject.

'Well, since you're talking about Norwich Union, let me tell you this. If you compare the discount they give when you insure both buildings and contents....'

But at this point Sashok stopped listening to Harry's constant droning, the more so because he spoke in a dreadful south London accent which was difficult to understand without serious concentration. And Sashok was tired.... He looked at Harry and thought: 'Now there sits a normal man, no longer young, not particularly successful in life, maybe a burglar, maybe not, perhaps just a retired insurance agent who has been slandered by town gossip. But this man is on his way home to his wife and children, to a nice meal, a glass of wine or a can of beer and then an evening with the family watching the latest serial on TV He'll get off the train and set off home to enjoy life's simple pleasures. And I? What awaits me? A hostile silence, that's what. A sad and upset wife. And what is more, Anna-Maria would most likely have given her parents to understand that she and Sashok had had a disagreement. And I will have no shoulder to cry on unless of course I phone Gavrilov in Moscow - he might be able to sympathise.'

But as he was approaching the house in his downcast state, Sashok was seized by another thought. Why exactly should he put his tail between his legs? After all, Anna-Maria did not know about Anastasia or about what had happened that day in the Cornwall Hotel. Her grumble with Sashok was just because of the strange events of the previous day, when he had made that stupid phone-call and then was brought home in a mysterious posh limousine. and because of a slight smell of whisky. In other words, for something that was no way his fault. Which meant in turn that she was taking offense unfairly and Sashok himself could quite reasonably strike a pose of offended dignity. And so he walked into the house with his head held high.

But there was a surprise waiting for Sashok. Anna-Maria, for the first time in her life apparently, had not come home the previous night.

CHAPTER THIRTEEN

The disappearing wife

It just did not seem possible as nothing like this had ever happened before. On those rare occasions when Anna-Maria was held up at work or when her social security department was organising some kind of event in support of a charity (such as a choir concert in aid of bats in Wales) she always gave plenty of prior warning. This meant that everybody knew well in advance that Anna-Maria was going to be late home and the forthcoming event was widely discussed within the family. But today she was not at home and this time the most surprising thing was that John and Maggie did not have a clue as to the whereabouts of their daughter.

'Sasha, don't you know where Anna-Maria is?' asked Maggie, with lowered eyes. Sashok knew his mother-in-law well enough to understand that it did not come easily to her to ask the question. And if she resorted to such extreme behaviour then he could safely assume that she was highly alarmed. John, it goes without saying, could not allow himself such emotional frankness but he did settle himself down in the adjacent kitchen while Maggie and Sashok were engaged in their conversation. And here you have a good example of the so called English hypocrisy: never mind that Sashok would guess that John, to put it crudely, was eaves-dropping. The only important thing for John was a formal 'alibi' an explanation, however improbable, but an explanation nevertheless. Hence the decision to wash dishes which were already clean. After all they could have picked up some dust since they were last washed 30 minutes ago, couldn't they? Moreover, it was absolutely imperative that Sashok understood what was going on, that no real deception was intended. Otherwise why do you suppose John was clattering the plates so loudly? Of course, to warn Sashok that his father-in-law was listening too, but pretending that he wasn't. All for the sake of convention. And it had to be done without making it too obvious. Gentlemen, of course, never engage in eavesdropping. On the other hand, one should never reveal one's anxiety and curiosity. All in all it was a clear case of double- or even triple-entry book-keeping. Sashok was quite fond of exploring these labyrinths but today, to be honest, he was not in the mood for the paradoxes of the English mind.

'Maggie,' said Sashok with a hint of desperation in his voice, 'I don't know where Anna-Maria is. She hasn't given me any indication of anything.'

And he made a big motion with his hands, forgetting for a second that his mother-in-law found such gestures shocking.

A second's pause followed. Maggie froze. And John froze in the kitchen. Through the half-open door Sashok could see him standing stock-still by the kitchen sink.

Then his mother-in-law and father-in-law got a grip of themselves.

'I'm sure she's just been held up at work and hasn't had a chance to warn us,' Maggie said in an artificially indifferent tone of voice. John could not restrain himself any longer and came into the dining room saying,

'No, of course, there's no need to worry.'

'If Anna–Maria doesn't come home they won't sleep a wink and they'll make themselves sick with worry but they will never let you see it,' thought Sashok.

But in point of fact he was the only one in the family who had grounds to suppose that there really was no need to get worked up about anything. Anna-Maria had probably just decided to teach him a lesson. Nevertheless it was bit unfair, he thought, given that she knew nothing about his real sins! She could have no inkling of what had gone on between him and Anastasia, the amazing Russian lady for whom he had reluctantly agreed (and under pressure) to act as a guide.

As for guiding in the strict sense of the word, well he hadn't got as far as that, because.... Yes, he had lost his head, got carried away.... Is it really possible to fall in love with an exact copy of your own wife and, if so, should that be considered to be infidelity?

While Sashok was engaged in these thoughts, John and Maggie took themselves off to bed as though nothing had happened.

Then the telephone rang.

'Hi, Sash,' said Anna-Maria's voice cheerily. 'How are things?'

'Hello,' answered Sashok, stunned. 'Everything's OK.... I'm fine.... And you?'

'I'm OK too.... We've got tons of work to do. We had to stay late. And I decided to spend the night at Laura's.'

'But tomorrow, you'll be home tomorrow?'

'I don't know yet.... It all depends....'

'But you'll phone?'

'We'll see.... I'll call you if...if I decide to come home. That is I mean, I mean if there isn't so much work.'

'If there isn't so much work,' Sashok repeated, vacantly.

'Can you tell my parents that I won't be coming home for the next few days?'

'Yes, OK, but can you give me Laura's phone number, just in case?'

'Sorry, but that would be awkward. Good bye for now!' said Anna-Maria and hung up.

This common English expression 'good bye for now' seemed terse and even hurtful in this context. 'To hell with you!' was Sashok's response. It was the first time in his life that he had been rude to Anna-Maria even though he hadn't at this point said it out loud.

Now Sashok was faced with the most repulsive task of conveying the unpleasant news to his parents-in-law. He tried at first of course to put it off by pottering about the house. He ate some fish and chips. Then he watched the BBC News on television and brushed his teeth. But it was getting late and whether he liked it or not he was going to have to go upstairs and knock on his in-laws' bedroom door. But as luck would have it Maggie herself suddenly came downstairs. Sashok guessed that the out-of-hours filling of the paper recycling bag was just an awkward excuse. From the expression on his mother-in-law's face it was obvious that she was struggling with a burning desire to ask the obvious question: 'Was that Anna-Maria who phoned?'

'Anna-Maria just phoned' said Sashok, 'she's asked me to tell you that she's up to her eyes in work and has decided to spend the night at Laura's.'

'Who's Laura?'

'I suppose someone in her department at work.'

'Have you never seen her?'

'No, I've only heard her. She sometimes phones us here'

'How very strange. I hope, Anna-Maria will be coming home tomorrow, then?' asked Maggie.'

'She doesn't know yet. It depends how much work she's got to do.'

'So what on earth does that....?' His mother-in-law started saying in surprise, but then she broke off. 'But of course. Naturally. Good night, Alexander.'

Sashok's mother-in-law seldom called him Alexander and it was usually a sign of some disapproval or, at least, disquiet. 'Well that's that, now she knows that things are not right between Anna-Maria and me' Sashok thought, resigning himself to the situation.

'Good night, Maggie, and I hope tomorrow will be a happier day for all of us.' he said.

'I'm counting on it,' Maggie muttered. Sashok wanted to show that he was genuinely playing according to English rules and if it didn't come out quite right, then it was not through want of trying. Here you are: without putting it into so many words, I am saying, in your English way, that I too am worried and I am acknowledging that things are not so wonderful; I am also prepared to humbly accept your displeasure with me, but I am hoping for the best and in any case I value your sympathy and tact.

But the truth was that inside Sashok's mind a storm was raging. Who could he turn to for advice? Whose shoulder could he cry on? Vugar's? Tsveta's? No, you don't talk to your work colleagues about this kind of thing. Should he call his mother in Yaroslavl? Certainly not! She would only get upset, her blood pressure would rise, she'd have palpitations and in any case, rather than help, she would only make things more complicated. What's the use of it? She'd do like she did last year, try to persuade him to pack everything in and come back to mother Russia and to home.

'If push comes to shove I may indeed end up cutting and running,' Sashok thought to himself gloomily. Then it suddenly dawned on him: you don't have to change the course of your life just to speak to your friends nor do you have to take an expensive flight to Moscow. There's electronic mail and even the telephone. True, it's difficult to pour out your soul by e-mail, and it's a bit late to call Gavrilov; it's already after midnight in Moscow. But Gavrilov is always out somewhere until late in the evening, so he may not be asleep yet. Anyway, he has to forgive his school pal, now in torment in a foreign land, for phoning him at an ungodly hour.

True it was not going to be very pleasant admitting the stupid things he'd done and Gavrilov would not miss the opportunity to laugh at Sashok, but on the other hand this man of the world would know what to advise him. Yes, phoning Gavrilov was a brilliant idea. Why hadn't Sashok thought of it before?

Especially as, somewhere in his bedside cabinet he had a phone card from Alfa or some such firm, which allowed incredibly cheap phone calls to Russia. But first of all Sashok went into John's study and booted up the PC (his father-in-law had already solemnly announced that Sashok could use both the study and the computer at any time) and sent Gavrilov an email which said, 'if you're not asleep, dear friend, would it not be possible to talk to you on the phone about something important?.'

Not only was Gavrilov not asleep but he must have been roaming in cyberspace because the reply came very quickly: 'Go ahead'.

Sashok ran into the bedroom to fetch his phone card and within a few seconds was listening to the inimitable nasal voice of his old mate.

'Well what's up, oh inhabitant of Albion? Why all of a sudden?'

'Valyera, listen, something pretty horrible is happening to me and I need you advice. The situation's like this....'

And Sashok, taking a deep breath, started to tell the whole painful story - apart from the bits he had already decided to leave in brackets.

Gavrilov reacted sluggishly; he sounded as if he was half asleep after all. Occasionally he expressed surprise but it seemed to Sashok that his reaction lacked sincerity. Mostly he just uttered indiscernible grunts. Sometimes he said nothing and Sashok would begin to worry that the line had gone down and he'd shout,

'Hello, hello... Valyera, can you hear me?'

To which Gavrilov answered,

'I can hear you alright, I haven't gone away.'

'What you have to understand,' Sashok was getting agitated, 'is that first of all they gave me a fake briefcase, then a fake copy of my wife. Tell me, what is the meaning of this fantasm?'

Gavrilov yawned down the phone and said:

'Sorry, old chap, lack of sleep's catching up with me... It looks like you are in the middle of some kind of Russian "happening". And you're dealing with somebody with a huge sense of humour. But it's not quite as simple as that, that's obvious; it's not being done just for the fun of it. I think, maybe, they're establishing a route.'

'What do you mean - a route?'

'For smuggling girls.... Human trafficking.... you know about it?'

'What are you saying? That would mean that this girl, Anastasia ... then she is a ....'

Gavrilov sniggered maliciously.

'Oh, I see, that's what is bothering you most! At least she's not your ordinary whore. At the very minimum she's one of the big bosses who's come out into the world.'

'So what should I do? Go to the police?'

'Don't even think about it! You're implicated now. You did accept money, didn't you? So under anybody's laws you are an accomplice. They'll send you to jail as sure as eggs is eggs, or if by any chance they don't, they'll throw you out of the country as an undesirable alien. Then, when you get back to Russia, these people will come looking for you. And they won't let you off the hook after you give them away. In a word, I'd strongly advise you not to. And on top of everything else ... this woman, what's her name ... Nadya?'

'Nastya....'

'OK, Nastya.... You slept with her, didn't you?'

'How do you know that?!' Sashok gasped.

'It's pretty obvious from the story you're telling. Remember Engels? 'A tendency derives from an action without any special indications....' So there you are.... Your Anna–Maria will never forgive you this 'tendency' and you know it.'

'God, what am I to do, then?'

'Just keep calm and the problem will resolve itself. I have a feeling the boys used you but now they don't need you anymore,' said Gavrilov.

After this the conversation went on aimlessly for a while. Sashok felt obliged to make the usual enquiries about Gavrilov's parents and discovered that his mother was ill but his father, once a big noise in some extremely secret department in the KGB 'still does a bit of work for his former employer on the side.' But Sashok was now hardly listening: his old friend displayed a kind of sleepy indifference towards him, and his advice was useless.

But then it has to be said that Sashok was less than frank with his old friend. He had not confided in him that he had another meeting with Anastasia planned for the following day. She had invited him to go with her to the Russian club to listen to a rock-group from St. Petersburg that was all the rage. It was a big event for the Russian colony in London and tickets were difficult to come by... but somehow Nastya had managed it.

CHAPTER FOURTEEN

Dancing with Russian wolves

The queue began on Oxford Street and snaked its way along the pavement forcing passers-by to avoid it by walking in the road. The snake hissed, laughed and swore in Russian and English and Sashok froze, dumbstruck, gazing at the fantastic spectacle.

'Come on, come on,'' said Anastasia, pulling him by the sleeve, 'they'll let us in, we don't need to queue.'

It was obvious that Nastya felt very much in her element here as if it was she, and not Sashok, who had lived in England for a good eight years and was now showing a novice what was what and where. She had managed to acquire a staggering Bordeaux-coloured suede coat and an almost aristocratic bearing which made her a different, rather haughty and inaccessible lady. And even the similarity to Anna-Maria was now not so obvious. Sashok began to feel somewhat timid in her presence, not least because she made an obvious impression on all those around her. It was surprising but even this queue, made up of self-satisfied beautiful people with long legs and bright clothes, smelling of expensive perfume and aftershave, suddenly fell silent and stared at Nastya. 'Wow!' someone said so that everyone could hear. Sashok did not manage to spot who it was exactly who said it, but he was in no doubt; the exclamation was directed at his companion. In situations like this simpler kinds of Englishmen regard it as a duty to whistle in a rumbustious, rollicking sort of way, and the local girls, depending on the degree of political correctness instilled in them in their childhood, take this either as a high compliment or a base insult. But the queue was mainly made up of Russians with some sprinkling of Russophiles and lovers of the exotic all of whom had no connection whatever with those classes, so none of them would have whistled. And thank heaven for that as Anastasia probably would have taken it the wrong way, while the expressive cry 'wow' needs no translation.... It's the same in England, Africa and even Moscow.

The entrance to the club, fenced off by a metal barrier, was guarded by feral-looking men in leather jerkins. But suddenly, the steel barrier opened and the bouncers meekly moved aside to let Nastya pass. She even didn't have to take two red velvet tickets, bearing the gold letters VIP, out of her handbag. Sashok trailed behind her, as if spell-bound, and could feel the suspicious eyes following him as if to say 'and what's that one doing here?' The faces of the bouncers dashed past him but one of them, a rather heavily builtblack man, suddenly seemed familiar to Sashok and the alarming thought flashed across his mind: 'Surely that can't be Dynkin?' But no, the face, was contorted in the characteristically local grimace as it erupted with a flood of swear words pronounced in the inimitable accent of South London, and Sashok immediately relaxed. The thug looked Sashok straight in the eye for a moment and seemingly wanted to say something but changed his mind and just waved him past as if to say, 'go in, then, since you've been so lucky.'

Under the fixed stare of the people in the queue Sashok and Anastasia passed through the steel doors where more courteous doormen searched handbags and briefcases which then had to be left in the cloakroom. Here another queue had formed where even the fortunate couple had to stand and they were immediately engulfed by the sound of Anglo-Rus. This word, with the stress on the second syllable, was Sashok's term for the strange language spoken among themselves (partly consciously and partly without realising it) by those of his countrymen who had been living in Britain for a long time. Sashok had sometimes entertained the idea of writing a popular study on the difference between Anglo-Rus and Runglish, the mixture of Russian and American English as spoken in Brighton Beach. What an interesting book that would make!

But Sashok didn't have time for philological investigations. He had to slave away for the merciless Indian Mr Singh, the publisher, and now he had to go with Nastya to the dreadful night club. 'But why, exactly, did you have to?' What was it exactly that made it a necessity?' his little inner voice asked. 'I have to, and that's all there is to it,' Sashok answered sternly. 'And I've no time to talk to you now. We'll speak later.' His inner voice felt offended and did not utter another word for a long time.

At the same time there was no shortage of other loud voices. One might even say that he was surrounded by such a din that he could hardly make out the remnants of conversation assailing his ears from all directions. A lanky, fidgety blond lad arm-in-arm with two tipsy young girls dressed all in black said something unbelievably funny to them, and repeating 'Cool, cool, of course, khorosho, kruto! Don't get in a sweat, nye par'tes', be happy!' Another gentleman whose appearance indicated his ancestors came from the southern parts of the Russian Empire somewhere in the Caucasus was trying to persuade his pale-complexioned girl-friend not to go back to 'khrenov fuckin GAP' again because it was a 'boring, skuchniy shop' with nothing worth having in it. Someone behind Sashok was explaining to his friends that he had not been in the club for ages because, for a whole month, he had been 'bolen, kak popugay, - 'as sick as a parrot' - using an expression which made no sense in Russian. And the possessor of a soft tenor voice for some reason was telling people, and almost boasting about it, that 'his sister sletela s ruchki - had flown off the handle.' In the meantime a naiad with luxuriant golden hair in the cloakroom was enquiring of her friends if she could 'poborovat' (borrow) their mirror. Behind her loomed a very tall, skinny youth with a shaven head who was complaining about some character called Semyonov: 'Can you imagine; he just vzyal i zakryl na menya dver' (went and closed the door on me).' Translated almost literally into Russian – with a bewildering result.

The club premises resembled a deep basement in which there was a stage and a huge hall without any armchairs or seats. 'That's OK,' thought Sashok, 'after all, it's for dancing, not watching shows.' Nevertheless, to his great relief, the VIP lounge was situated in an area behind a glass partition overlooking the hall and was well equipped with tables and chairs. And, more importantly, the thick glass which divided the lounge from the dance floor, as soon became clear, protected his ears from the shock wave emanating from the huge speakers below which were several times taller than the average man. Sashok was able to appreciate this advantage only some time later.

When she had settled herself down at a table Anastasia sent Sashok off to fetch the drinks. For some reason there were no waiters even in the VIP lounge and everyone had to go and stand in a queue, pay and then carry the drinks back to the table.

'A Tequila Sunrise for me,' ordered Anastasia. Then she cast a doubting glance at Sashok and added politely, in an almost inaudible voice, 'let me give you some cash.'

Sashok took heated offence.

'Certainly not! I'm not out of work and I am not living on benefits,' he said proudly and made his way to the bar.

But when he got to the end of the queue he did begin to wonder how he was going to pay for the cocktails. As usual he had no ready cash on him apart from the miserable two pounds reserved for his sandwich. But he did have his 'Switch' debit card which drew on his and his wife's joint account and which he only used very rarely. Of course, Anna-Maria would raise her eyebrows in surprise when she saw this unexpected expenditure on the bank statement, but then – in for a penny, in for a pound! What will be, will be, but today he had to maintain his dignity. The most important thing at the moment was whether or not they accepted these cards in bars. He would be ashamed to have to go back to Anastasia with his tail between his legs and, cringing with embarrassment, ask her for money (only a loan, of course, but still a source of shame). However, the effeminate youth with his hair in a pigtail and an ear-ring in his right ear (Sashok, to be honest, had forgotten which ear showed what sexual orientation) grunted unsympathetically and went to find the machine.

The queue behind him was by now growing annoyed and tut-tutting, irritated by the wait. Sashok entered his pin, trying not to look at the amount (no point getting upset about it now) and solemnly carried two smart-looking glasses, containing a pale pink, slightly foaming beverage, in outstretched hands back to his table. To tell the truth, the cocktails tasted worse than they looked, and the alcohol went straight to his head. Otherwise he would not have made it so easy for Anastasia to take him down to the dance floor.

At first all that could be heard from the other side of the glass partition was a recording, a vague cross between R&B and house music (Sashok could hardly tell the difference). And the volume was bearable; he and Anastasia could even carry on an intimate conversation. But when 'The Blinis' appeared on stage to the sound of whistling, whooping and shouting, it was as if the world had exploded. Now it was virtually impossible to carry on talking.

And that was when Nastya took hold of Sashok, who was by now the worse for wear, and asked him to dance. He was not ready for such a turn of events. But Anastasia was not prepared to take 'no' for an answer and grabbed him by the hand (Sashok had to admit that this was extremely pleasant) and dragged him down to where people were dancing. But God, what was it like down there! The noise from the speakers drowned out not only all other sounds – it was impossible to distinguish any tune. There were only mind-numbing, gut-churning bass sounds and screeching, brain-drilling high notes as well as the suffocating cast-iron beat of the drums. And all this failed to blend into anything which could possibly be described as harmonious. But for the many-headed creature swaying about in time to the noise in the semi-gloom, it was a kind of 'high.' At first Sashok was afraid that he would not be able to last out, that he would faint and collapse in a heap or, worse than that, that he would be sick right in front of everybody's eyes. But, as it turned out, he managed somehow to get a grip of himself and even started moving in time with the beat. His hearing might be damaged and would take some time to recover, but what the hell. God willing it would be restored. Gradually Sashok got carried away, let his hair down.

Although he would never admit it, deep down inside Sashok loved to dance and was not too bad at it. In this field his education was minimal – a mere six weeks in a dance group, but he always came out top in eurhythmics in primary school. The young teacher told his mother that he had natural rhythm and remarkable physical coordination. His mother later conveyed these compliments to Sashok, laughing as she did so; she was not sure herself whether or not to be proud of these talents. 'If only you were as good at mathematics,' she concluded. And this comment hit the nail on the head. Sashok was quite a good student in the humanities but in drawing, sketching and geometry he had problems. 'Deficient in space awareness,' said his uncle Michael with a sigh. He assumed that this defect was inherited and perhaps due to his genetic makeup. It could be partially compensated for by rigid training, but only partially. If God did not give you a gift then there was very little you could do about it. In compensation, he was given other talents like his natural rhythm and dancing abilities. But why were those talents bestowed upon him? Was there a reason? Maybe to impress a stunningly beautiful woman called Anastasia (who bore a mystifying resemblance to his wife) on the dance floor in a Russian nightclub?

In his normal life he had precious few opportunities to display this talent of his, mainly because Anna-Maria was not a particularly good dancer and was not too keen on dancing. But Anastasia was something else! As her lithe body twisted and glided from movement to movement it seemed as though it wasn't her who was dancing in time to the music but the music itself that was following her every movement, adapting itself to the contractions of her muscles. Moreover, Sashok felt that he was submerging into something like a dialogue with his irresistible partner which was not without its erotic subtext. He was getting more and more ecstatic as something amazing, tender and magical swelled within his breast. In fact he got so carried away that he did not notice that Nastya had disappeared!

Literally a second earlier he had been looking through the gloom and the flickering coloured lights into her magnetic eyes and, between Sashok and Anastasia, it seemed, there shimmered, gleamed and flashed an invisible connecting thread. And suddenly – snap!- the thread broke. Sashok had just completed a complicated, improvised pirouette and then in the blink of an eye he had lost sight of his partner.... There she was and then ... gone! For another couple of seconds Sashok, not knowing what to do, continued to move in time with the rhythm, squeezed in from all sides by the swaying crowd and back to back with a plumpish blond in white leather trousers. He turned his head in all directions trying to work out where Nastya had disappeared to, but in the half-light, visibility was limited.

'She's probably gone to the toilet, the lavatory,' Sashok thought, trying to remember which term should be used in the given context. You see, in England the correct term for 'the toilet' is an important clue about social standing and a sort of password which divides one group of people from another. In polite society God help you if you say 'toilet' instead of 'lavatory'.....people will think you're a slob. On the other hand, among unpretentious people 'lavatory' will mark you down as a snob. Among the younger intelligentsia the most widely used brief expression, of mysterious origin, is 'loo.' But these people also use the term 'John' jokingly (if one can joke about such matters). In common daily use it is simpler to use the expression 'the gents' (i.e. the place for the gentlemen) and its equivalent 'the ladies.' In a lower-middle-class environment, or when talking to waiters, the preferred word is 'bathroom.' But here, in a Russian nightclub, such nuances are of no particular significance, so any Russian expression would be all right as well as any of the afore-mentioned English terms. But the use here of more proletarian expressions like 'ubornaya', ('the bog') would give rise to fastidious giggles.

'You didn't notice where my girl friend went, did you?' Sashok asked a woman in white, smiling stupidly. In reply the blond only shrugged a sloping shoulder and, roaring 'let's dance' grabbed him by the hand and pulled him into her circle of dancers.

Sashok jerked about flaccidly in the circle of two unknown men and three girls. Nastya was nowhere to be seen.

Here, inside the Leviathan, the club seemed to be unbelievably huge and the crowd, heaving to the sound of the deafening music, resembled a beast with a thousand arms and legs, shaking all over the place and yelling from a thousand throats. And the crowd was illuminated from above with green, red and yellow light. Everybody around Sashok seemed so joyful and friendly and then suddenly somebody stood painfully on his foot.

'Oops, I'm so sorry. I do apologize, please forgive me…. I didn't mean to….' muttered Sashok, trying to cope with his sore foot.

'You're not sorry at all, so don't apologize,' some fearsome type answered, and Sashok suddenly felt sharp pain in his other foot.

'Ouch!' Sashok exclaimed not too loudly, 'Oh, you didn't have to do that, why….'

'I am going to show you why….'

Only now did Sashok begin to understand what was going on. While he was waving his arms and legs about, the hot blonde's partner had come back from the toilet (or lavatory). She, possibly, had decided to tease her fancy man a bit and had deliberately pressed herself up against Sashok just at the moment when he returned. The fancy man appeared to have no sense of humour and was now getting ready to give Sashok a good working over.

'No, you've misunderstood, it was an accident,' babbled Sashok, 'I came here with another girl! She went off somewhere for a second and she'll be back any moment now. I swear I had no intention of….'

'I'll give you intention,' answered the wild man, and Sashok found it hard not to yell out, so painful was the way the wild man stood on his already aching left foot.

The wild man turned out to be a complete professional when it came to foot-stamping. He maintained his rhythmic dance movement and at every third beat he conducted a strike on Sashok's feet.

'Now let's see if you can dance,' he said, with a grim smirk.

The pain was becoming completely unbearable. Sashok tried several times to turn away, and half of the time he managed it, but not managing it the other half was more than enough. 'I soon won't have any feet left!' he thought, panic-stricken. So what else was there for him to do? Retreat in shame? Impossible! Stand on the yob's feet in return? Madness! So in absolute desperation, unaware of what he was doing, Sashok suddenly barked,

'You oaf! Let's go outside and sort this out!'

'Fuck you, mat' tvoyu, let's!' the aggressor roared, only too happy to oblige.

CHAPTER FIFTEEN

The deadly duel

As they were walking to the door the blond in the leather trousers tried to stop her dance partner and persuade him not to get into a fight. 'Borya, Bobochka' she whispered, sidling up to him, 'you mustn't; this guy had nothing to do with it. I was having a little joke.... It turned out wrong.... What's the point of smashing the chairs?'

'To hell with the chairs.....I'm going to break something else.....you'll know not to joke next time,' Boris snapped sullenly, clearly intending to teach his girlfriend a lesson with a punch in the face. It was clear, though, that the face chosen for the punch wouldn't be hers but somebody else's. And it was not difficult to guess whose exactly.

'Come on then, hurry up!' hissed Bobochka evilly, trying to push Sashok forward. 'Get your bloody hands off me!' Sashok snapped back indignantly. He was determined to defend his dignity. He wasn't a coward; he was going to fight come what may. But it wasn't going to be easy. The brute's hands seemed to be made of iron. Sashok was trying hard not to allow panic to overwhelm him: he had decided to get to the door with his self-respect intact, and then consider his options. Why panic in advance? Who could tell how things would turn out? After all, the bouncers might decide to get involved. And the appearance of the police was a possibility, too. Or Boris's friends (if they were indeed his friends) might try and restrain their overwrought comrade. And there was another thing too. When they were making their way to the door it became clear that Boris had been quite seriously drinking. On the one hand, this was bad news; under the influence of alcohol a Russian's brakes often fail (it can happen to Englishmen too!). On the other hand, this could turn out to be good news, as a drunken fighter is not very good with his fists. And what about his legs and feet? There was no denying that Boris was quite good at stomping on other people's limbs on the dance floor, but he seemed to have staggered a couple of times on the stairs. 'Ah,' thought Sashok, rather pleased, 'it would appear that the last tot of whisky is beginning to take effect!'

Outside it was raining but Sashok and Boris emerged from the club with no coats on. 'Oh well, this should sober him up,' thought Sashok, who then said, 'Listen, Boris, all this is senseless. If I've offended you unintentionally, I'm prepared to offer my apologies.'

Boris took stock, thought about the situation and then took a firm decision.

'I don't give a shit for your apologies. Walk on a bit, let's go further away.'

Sashok moved slowly towards a dark back street and as he did so he glanced at the security men standing by the club door. One of them (possibly the black man who bore a resemblance to Dynkin) looked over and waved at Sashok, and then calmly turned his back on him. The plump blonde who was the cause of the business had also disappeared. And this is what happened next.

As soon as Sashok found himself alone with Boris, the latter unleashed a torrent of profanities but his swearing came mixed with strange wailing and incantations as if he were intoning a prayer or exorcizing devils ('he's cranking himself up, that's what he is doing' thought Sashok). Finally he decided to kick Sashok from behind, in the kidneys, but he was unable to invest his kick with full physical and moral strength. It was if he was doing it without a will, without conviction. Almost despite himself, because he felt obliged to. Possibly this was because the quantity of Glenlivet in his bloodstream had reached a critical level. In a word, Boris looked exhausted. And somehow, Sashok's managed to guess the exact moment and direction of the blow. It was as though someone was whispering something in his ear. At the very last moment he jumped quickly to the right and his adversary's foot whizzed past his side, missing by a few millimeters.

Boris now had a problem: he was wearing shoes which were quite unsuitable in bad weather for such activity. To be sure, they were a smart pair of shoes (Churchill or Russell and Bromley), with thin soles, really classy, and must have cost a fortune, but they were totally useless when it came to rapid movements on wet asphalt. The same could not be said about the cheap 'Hush Puppies' Sashok had worn to the club as he had nothing more suitable. And then alcohol, even in the most solid of men, has an adverse effect on physical coordination. So, to cut a long story short, when he missed his aim, Boris could not maintain his balance on one leg and landed with a thump on the asphalt. He saw stars as the back of his head hit the ground.

He lay motionless for some time. Sashok stood to one side and just looked at him, not knowing what to do. Then he even began feeling concerned about his adversary's health. He took the decision to come a bit closer, and asked, cautiously,

'Are you all right?'

Boris did not say a word.

'Perhaps I should call a doctor,' suggested Sashok.

But no sooner had he bent over the prostrate figure than it moved. And not only moved; Bobochka immediately came out with vicious threats, promising alternatively, to bury Sashok or to cut his balls off. Sashok thought it wise to move slightly away. And he was right to do so, because Boris got up, first onto his knees and then, with obvious difficulty, on to his feet.

'Now you're going to cop it, you shit,' he yelled in a strange, cracked voice. Then he rushed at Sashok.

Sashok just had time to turn round and tear off. God, could he run! He was no slower than in his old college days when he took part in track and field events, mainly because it offered a way out from boring PT classes. This time he had to run a tight circle in the side street where not long before people had stood in a queue to get into the club. Boris plodded along in his wake. The distance between the two was gradually growing, until Sashok started closing on Boris from behind. Sashok was forced to slow down a bit so as not to catch up with his adversary.

And that is when Sashok suddenly noticed that Boris's breathing sounded very odd: it was irregular and hoarse.

'Oi, Boris, stop running like that,' Sashok could not help shouting, 'you'll do yourself an injury. You've got a problem with your breathing. If only you could see yourself! Believe me, you need medical help. It's not worth carrying on like this,' shouted Sashok as he ran.

But Boris took his genuine concern for an attempt to humiliate him and, making a u-turn, put his head down and charged Sashok like a rugby player, trying to grab his legs. Sashok just had time to react. Literally at the last moment, a fraction of a second before contact was made, he jumped clear and Boris's hands slid under the heels of Sashok's Hush Puppies. Sashok fell over clumsily, and struck Boris with his shoe, either on the temple or on the ear. Whatever the case, Boris let out a frightening yell and grabbed his head in his hands.

'You shit!' he screamed

This time it was a good five minutes before Boris could get up. Sashok, fascinated, followed his awkward movements and watched as he swayed and turned his powerful frame, looking for Sashok with dimmed eyes. Sashok had never seen anything like it. 'He's in a groggy state' was the boxing term that came into his head. For some reason he no longer felt frightened and when Boris, gathering what remained of his strength, turned on him again, Sashok effortlessly and elegantly, like a real bull-fighter, swerved nimbly to the side so that the furious beast passed him on his left hand side. And he even surprised himself when he heard himself saying, in a loud voice, 'Whoa there!' But at the same time he felt ashamed because Boris, missing his target, smashed head first into the steel barrier which still stood in the side street even though the queue had now gone. He immediately let out a sort of plaintive cry and then just lay on the wet ground.

Having learned from bitter experience, Sashok did not go near him. Standing at a safe distance he tried to persuade Boris to agree to calling for medical help. But he made no reply and just groaned quietly. Then, as if from nowhere, the blonde in white leather reappeared.

'What have you done to him!' she shouted, bending over Boris, 'his face is all smashed in!'

'I didn't do anything. It's just very slippery round here,' said Sashok in an attempt to explain the situation.

But the blonde was in no mood to listen.

'You didn't need to be so cruel. Even if he was in the wrong, it wasn't necessary to beat the man half to death!'

At this point Boris's friends appeared.

'He's covered in blood, his eye brow's split and it looks as if his nose is broken. We'll have to call an ambulance,' said one of them who, by all appearances, had a medical background.

'And the police, too,' added another, staring meaningfully at Sashok.

'But you don't understand, he simply had a bad fall,' said Sashok as he tried to edge closer to the people standing around the motionless body. But they shuffled timidly to the side.

Only the blonde came striding valiantly towards Sashok.

'Don't you think that's enough for today?' she said angrily, 'or are you after more blood?

Sashok did not know what to reply to this, not least because a large crowd had now gathered. The club bouncers also turned up, and one of them started talking into his mobile phone. 'He's calling for the law,' thought Sashok, horrified. And then someone grabbed Sashok by the arm and whispered into his ear:

'What are you standing there like that for? Have you gone mad? It's time to clear off!'

Sashok turned round: it was Nastya!

'Where did you get to,' he asked sternly.

'Never mind that now. We've got to get out of here.'

It was amazing the way Anastasia was able to pull Sashok out of the crowd which timidly made way for her.

'Here, put this on.'

Surprisingly, Anastasia had managed to somehow get hold of Sashok's coat!

'But I've still got the ticket!'

'Don't worry. They won't miss it. Now let's go!'

Sashok had no choice but to submit to the fearless Amazon.

CHAPTER SIXTEEN

The things they do in Soho

Nastya took Sashok by the hand and led him through the London night until they came to the fleshpot depths of Soho. It seemed to Sashok that he had never been here before or perhaps it was just that everything looked so different at night. All these places seemed to be very cheerful. There were lots of people, all laughing as though they didn't have a care in the world. They seemed to be heading somewhere purposefully and chit-chatting cheerfully about something as if the clock was pointing not to three o'clock in the morning but to some hour in the early afternoon. 'Surely these people have to sleep some time,' thought Sashok, shocked at what he was seeing, 'and surely they have to work sometimes, too.' But the really surprising thing was that there were very few drunks about or not too many people who were high on drugs. And, surprisingly, Sashok, although he was wandering through these streets at night, felt under no threat; there was nothing in the air to make him feel he was about to be attacked.

Occasionally Nastya stopped, looked around, muttered some street names under her breath and scrutinized a piece of paper.

'Where are we going?' enquired Sashok

'You'll soon see.... And you'll like it,' answered Nastya.

Eventually she found what she was looking for; an ordinary-looking, dirty beige-coloured two-storey building which was long overdue for a coat of paint. Its unattractive columns were in pseudo-classical style. It also had a portico but it too was rather unprepossessing. The sturdy wooden door was protected by moveable steel shutters which, presumably, could be opened and shut during non-working hours (that is to say, during the day). Over the door was a sign, in illuminated bold red letters, which said 'The Red Cockerel.' Nastya pressed a door-bell and the door opened immediately. A head, atop a bull neck, appeared and tiny, sleepy eyes flashed to the right and to the left as they observed Sashok's face......

'Hi, Bugor' said Nastya as she gave the bouncer one of her drop-dead-gorgeous smiles. And he in turn broke into a big, toothy grin.

'Hi, Nastya,' he said in Russian, with a thick southern accent. 'Long time no see. Come on in. Things are a bit quiet in here tonight.'

'Just you wait. We'll liven them up a bit.'

Bugor stood to one side. Behind the door was a steep staircase illuminated by the flickering dim red light from a wall-lamp. A warm, unfamiliar sweet and spicy smell emanated from below. Nastya led Sashok down the stairs and he meekly followed, thinking 'Wondrous are the ways of the Lord!' Well, perhaps not necessarily the Lord's'?

At the bottom of the stairs the red light was slightly brighter and the smell was stronger. There were few people about....just some couples sitting at the tables. A few men and women in brightly coloured clothes huddled around the bar.

'Welcome to the Red Cockerel!' said a tiny girl whose beauty was out of this world.

Why 'out-of-this-world'? Because creatures like her were not known to walk the face of the Earth! She was small, slender with enormous eyes which seemed, unbelievably, to cover half of her face. Sashok stared at her as if bewitched, thinking 'I can't imagine she could be sexually attractive to anyone on earth; but on Mars or Jupiter or what is the name of the planet she came from, it might be a different matter. There she could be phenomenally successful and might even cause a riot. And even here in London there might be a few people who would not mind putting such an exotically beautiful statuette on the mantelpiece. People would not be able to take their eyes off her!' But Sashok wouldn't have dared to do it as the statuette would have looked too much like a living woman. And then, he did not have a mantelpiece....

'We have a free table,' the girl from another planet chirped as she led them to a far corner where the clouds of heavy grey smoke made it very difficult to make out the free table amidst the claret-coloured leather settees.

'What would you like to drink?' asked the girl from Mars.

Sashok ordered a Tequila Sunrise, because he did not really have any idea what else people drank in bars like this. He knew that if he had gone for a 'gin and tonic' or 'whisky and soda' he really would be putting his foot in it and, to tell the truth, this had happened to him before. In the very early days of his life in England his father-in-law had invited Sashok to dine with him at his London club. It was all plush velvet and portraits of important gentlemen with double chins (all in gold frames and three times normal height). Highly disciplined attendants in smoking jackets or some other ancient form of dress served food and drinks.... Before dinner it was the custom to stand for a while at the bar while the table was being laid and the hors-d'oeuvres prepared. Sashok wanted to pass himself off as a refined gentleman and not a country bumpkin, so he asked for a cognac as an aperitif. And not just any old cognac, but a genuine French 'Napoleon'. But the first thing that soon became abundantly clear was that such a brand did not exist; it was a kind of sub-class shared by several products. The second thing was that cognac is drunk as an aperitif only by *zhloby* (this was the closest Russian translation Sashok could find for the beautiful English word 'slob'). Perhaps plumbers who gave up school early could also be included in this group. Sashok's father-in-law was somewhat embarrassed by the incident and never invited him to his club again. But this was a mistake. Sashok was a fast learner and he had picked up a lot of things since then. Like single-malt whisky as well as 'Merlot' and Australian 'Shiraz.' He would not make that kind of mistake again. But here, in this strange night spot it wasn't like John's club, it was different again. And, generally speaking, his memories of cocktails was very hazy; he recalled 'Champagne Cobler (or was it

Champagne Kleber?) from the old days of the Soviet Union, a kind of murky blue liquid. And then there was 'Northern Lights' – half cognac, half sweet Soviet Champagne. But all this belonged to a world now gone and best forgotten. So Sashok decided to suffer in silence and stay with his 'Sunrise' rather than experiment and risk his reputation. All the same, Nastya was a bit surprised at his choice.

'I thought you didn't like it,' she muttered. 'And anyway, tequila, that's yesterday's drink.'

'So what's in fashion now?' enquired Sashok.

'Well, I don't know.... Black Russian or Red Bull with vodka. Then there's strawberry Daikiri.... But that's more of a woman's drink.'

'Black Russian? That'll do! I might not be black but I am certainly Russian!'

'You'd be better having a Red Bull.... You're certainly no bull, but you might need some energy today.'

'What for?' Sashok asked cautiously.

'Can't you guess?'

Nastya leaned over the table and looked him straight in the eye so that he once again felt the magical electricity emanating from her. That sweet bliss of forbidden fruit penetrated every pore, coursed through his veins as if they were electric cables. He even got a lump in his throat so that he could say nothing in reply. He could only manage an inarticulate grunt. Then Nastya puckered her lips at him, but....

Right above his head Sashok heard a husky, purring voice,

'Do you mind if we join you?'

Sashok recoiled from Nastya, jumped up like a scalded cat, trying to understand where he was and what was going on.

A couple, total strangers, was standing by the table. Sashok's first reaction was to give a curt 'no'. Couldn't these people see that he and Nastya were tied up? Didn't they realise that the table was quite small and four people around it would be a bit of a squeeze? And, surely, there were other places free? But then maybe there weren't! Sashok stopped himself mid-sentence. And in any case he was not sure what course of action would be appropriate in this strange place. He looked at Anastasia, hoping she would come to his aid. She'd know how to deal with this ill-mannered couple. But the strange thing was that Nastya smiled charmingly at the new arrivals and even gestured to them to sit down at their table! Sashok looked at the man: he was a tall, lean blond with a huge, ugly Adam's apple. Surely women don't find men like that attractive? Then he looked at the lady with him: God, a dark-skinned mixed-race woman! That was really too much! Sashok was not a racist, he just had no experience of socialising with humans of different skin colour. On closer inspection he noticed her very long legs, crowned with a very short mini-skirt and also her bare, beautifully formed and magnificent, flawless shoulders. True, her shoulders were black, and this for some reason created a strange feeling; he was at a loss as to how to react to them. Her face, broad nose and extremely bushy hair seemed a bit wild to Sashok; but he was no connoisseur of black beauty. On the other hand the semi-transparent material that concealed her breasts (not very large, but high and erect) did have an effect on him. Obviously, there was no sign of any kind of bra, so that even in the semi-darkness her firm, resilient nipples stood proud and visible.

'Oh, oooooh,' was all Sashok could manage to say.

'Sit down, sit down, please,' said Nastya, smiling, but they were already taking their places and making themselves comfortable, without waiting for the gift of speech to return to Sashok.

Then the unreal waitress appeared again and took the new guests' orders. The man chose absinthe with ice and the black lady a Red Bull with vodka.

It turned out the Afro-British lady's name was Melanie and her lanky companion introduced himself by a strange-sounding name or pseudonym. Sashok nearly choked on his drink and, not believing his own ears, asked the man to say it again.

'Absolument,' the man with the large Adam's apple repeated nonchalantly.

'Isn't that the French for 'absolutely', 'completely?' enquired Sashok.

'Oh, yes, it is' he replied, nodding his head.
'Are you French, then?
'Definitely not.'
'But your name's ... *Absolument*?'
'Yes, but you may call me Jack.'

It became immediately obvious that 'Jack' intended to strike up a conversation with Nastya and the black girl Melanie was going to engage him, Sashok. But Nastya had a problem.... She knew *absolument* no English at all. All she could say was 'please,' 'thank you' and 'face control.' She is not going to get far with this vocabulary, thought Sashok, and thank heaven for that! But he was mistaken.

No more than a couple of minutes had passed and at the other end of the table communication was going ahead with no problems whatever. *Absolument* was whispering animatedly into Nastya's ear, and she was smiling back meaningfully, screwing up her beautiful eyes, as if she understood whatever was being said.

An unpleasant heavy feeling arose from the depths of Sashok's very being. For some reason he felt an unbearable urge to take the shoe off his left foot and beat Jack about the head with it. He remembered Boris from the Russian club: he did not do too badly with him in the end! 'If the worst comes to the worst, I might have a run-around with this one, too' the thought occurred to him. Meanwhile, the black lady was trying to attract Sashok's attention and was speaking to him in a flirty, husky voice which was not all that easy for Sashok to understand. 'Take it easy, weirdo. It's not you I am interested in,' Sashok said in Russian. But she did not understand and just smiled as she pressed her warm thigh against Sashok's knee. 'Now listen....' Sashok began, angrily, turning to face Melanie, but he immediately stopped short, stunned by the spectacle that confronted him. The dark girl for some reason had opened her mouth wide as if she was silently laughing at something. Until this point Sashok for some reason had always imagined that black persons' gums were black but now, on closer inspection, they turned out to be every bit as red as a white person's. And Melanie's tongue, which she was twirling and making clicking noises with, now flattening it, now twisting it like a ribbon, now sticking it out and moving its pointed end along her upper lip. This tongue was also completely red. For some reason this combination (the colour of chocolate tinged with red) held Sashok spell-bound. He suddenly caught himself staring fixedly and in an ill-mannered way at Melanie's tongue, at her enchantingly full lips and pearly white teeth. He suddenly forgot all about his left shoe and about cheeky Jack. He was seized by a powerful, inexplicable, irresistible and all consuming desire to touch this tongue with his lips and even give them a gentle bite. From somewhere deep down inside, his little voice said 'You, my friend, have gone totally mad.' But Sashok was no longer in any state to reply because his mouth was already in contact with Melanie's and her astonishing tongue was already deep inside and tenderly caressing the roof of his mouth.

'Hey cool it!' Nastya shouted at Sashok. Ashamed, he separated himself from Melanie and even moved away from her a bit. 'My God,' he thought, 'I should be ashamed of myself for losing my self-control like that.' But his inner voice said maliciously, 'It's not your day for kissing today; don't even think about it.' In the meantime the dark girl was saying something in her strange, unfamiliar accent. On the one hand she was using normal English words such as 'half', 'split', 'for', 'swap' but the way they were put together did not make any sense. She must have been using some special jargon. Or, maybe the problem was the feverish excitement which gripped Sashok and from which he could not escape. Jack meanwhile had also started to speak and he too was using strange incomprehensible words. 'Will you say that again, please?' Sashok asked. Jack obediently repeated the same unintelligible sounds and then Melanie chipped in and repeated the same words, emphasizing everything slowly the way people do when they are speaking to foreigners who are slow on the uptake. But there was a problem: her diction was not all that great. Or, perhaps, it was Sashok who had problems with his hearing. Then Melanie looked at his bewildered expression and burst out laughing. Jack quickly followed. A second later Anastasia joined in. Then

Sashok (what else could he do?) tried to force a laugh out of himself, too, but the result was not too convincing. Nastya looked at him suspiciously and then said,

'Right. OK, then. Make up your mind. Whatever you decide, we'll do.'

'Decide? Make up my mind? ' asked Sashok, stunned. 'Well, personally.... I don't know.'

'Come on. These people are waiting for an answer. Do you agree or not?'

Sashok turned his head and saw that Jack and Melanie were motionless with expectation and were looking at him impatiently.

'Agree? To what?' Sashok thought. A game of cards, move to another bar or going to somebody's house? Or to bet on who could drink the most vodka without any nibbles to eat? All these possibilities ran through Sashok's mind. Any of them seemed entirely plausible. What wasn't possible was to admit that he had completely ceased to comprehend spoken English. Added to this mystery, Anastasia on the contrary seemed to understand perfectly everything that was being said.... What the hell was going on? Sashok decided that he had to play for time or provoke them into saying something which would offer some kind of explanation.

'Well, I don't know,' he said dreamily, 'it all depends....'

'Depends on what?' Anastasia asked straight off.

'Well ... it depends.... Listen, can we have something to drink?'

'No problem.'

And Nastya called the extraterrestrial girl.

It was at this very moment that Sashok realised the root of his problems: the cocktails were going straight to his head! That was a serious mistake – to order a Black Russian after a Red Bull. Mixing them clearly was not a good move. An unhelpfully explosive concoction was forming inside his body.

But the remaining sober part of his consciousness noticed that Nastya, Jack and Melanie had quickly downed their cocktails and were now watching his glass and waiting. Sashok also looked at his glass at the bottom of which a few drops of the black liquid remained. 'I'm black and she's Russian.... No, it's the other way round. But it doesn't matter,' was the thought that flashed through his mind. Around the table silence reigned. Just one person was giggling quietly. 'It's me, I am giggling,' Sashok realised in astonishment. And the surprise made him laugh louder. Then he hiccupped and downed the rest of his cocktail in one go.

'Well, then, agreed?' asked Anastasia in Russian.

Sashok hiccupped again and said,

'OK ... agreeeed ... agreeed, whatever....'

'To the first or the second?'

'To both.'

And then he translated for Jack and Melanie: 'Both. I'd like to do both.'

Nastya frowned.

'I'm afraid you can't do both. Although ... what exactly did you mean?'

Meantime Jack and Melanie were having a lively debate about something. Then they both stood up. Jack gave the Martian some cash and whispered something in her ear. She nodded. Jack turned round and gestured with his hand as if to say 'follow me.' Then, making his way past the bar, he opened a half-hidden door. The people who were standing by the bar saw all this and for some reason started clapping.

'Come on, old misery!' said Anastasia taking a firm grip of Sashok's arm. 'Why have you gone to pieces after so little?'

'Where are we going?' asked Sashok.

'This place has got rooms upstairs.'

'What are we going to do there?'

'Both. I think we'll do both,' said Nastya, chuckling in a not very friendly kind of way.

'Perhaps it's not worth it? Can't we sit here a bit longer and have another drink?'

'*Pozdnyak metat'sya*' - it's too late to change your mind,' Anastasia announced assertively, using a very strange Russian expression he had not heard before, as she grabbed hold of his arm.

125

Sashok decided to submit to his fate. He went where the woman led him and he thought: 'How quickly the Russian language is changing! You spend a few years out of the country and before you know it *pozdnyak metat'sya* - that really is something.'

CHAPTER SEVENTEEN

The day after

Someone, with relentless and persistent cruelty, was hammering a walnut. The nut cracked but did not shatter. But the pain was simply awful.

This walnut turned out to be Sashok's head which, by some miracle, did not break under the blows. Gradually it became clear that there were no blows and no hammer, but that what Sashok was experiencing was the most dreadful hangover he had ever had in his life. And as well as the pulsating headache he also became aware of a semi-paralysis that was affecting his limbs. Worst of all was what was happening to his mouth and throat and to his ability to swallow. The whole passageway seemed to be on fire. For the first time in his life Sashok understood the meaning of the old Russian expression 'as if a squadron had spent the night in your mouth.' Previously he had just taken this to be a humorous, if absurd metaphor. But not so now. Now he felt as though a cavalry squadron had indeed spent the night in his mouth together with their horses... a very large number of horses.

With a tremendous effort Sashok opened his eyes a little. The bed and the whole room in which he woke up seemed unfamiliar, but then in his present condition he could not be sure of anything. A few seconds later he had the feeling that the room had turned on its axis and that he, Sashok, was somehow nailed to the ceiling along with the bed and his head was hanging upside down. But then a relatively normal perception of the world was re-established.... Or at least the ceiling and floor returned to their normal positions. It was now just the air that remained hazy as if held in a kind of chalky suspension.

In an armchair opposite him, and staring intently at him, sat a girl who looked very much like his wife. 'Anna Maria, at last, you've come back!' Sashok was on the point of blurting out, but at the last moment he choked on his words, so that what came out was nothing more than 'Anm....' It was a rather unusual interjection.

'What did you say?' the girl asked in Russian, laughing. 'Was that some exotic language?'

And it immediately became obvious that the girl was certainly not Anna-Maria. His wife could not have mastered Russian in the few days since he had seen her. The girl's manner was, on the whole, too relaxed and the negligee she was wearing was too risky. Very pale pink and completely transparent, revealing so much that the half-dead Sashok suddenly felt a twinge of desire.

'Lazarus has risen from the dead,' said Sashok. To be honest, his tongue was failing him and as a result he sounded really strange – as if he were speaking Russian with some foreign accent.

'Hey.... Have you by some chance been swapped for somebody else?' asked the girl in the negligee. 'You look different and you're speaking like a foreigner.... Are you pretending to be Estonian?'

Sashok had more or less worked out who this beauty was even though he did still harbour some doubts. For instance, had he not dreamed some parts of what had happened to him during the past few days? The events of last night he could not remember at all, and he found this very disturbing. Dark shadows drifted fleetingly across his mind as did snatches of incomprehensible phrases in various languages. He did not know if any of this had really happened or if it was all a dream. Then he suddenly remembered, very clearly, the man with the surprising name of *Absolument* and his sexy companion. He also remembered the strange Russian expression that the girl in front of him had used to tell him it was too late to change his mind. There was no doubt about it: this was no dream. The mental strain caused the hammer to descend once more onto the walnut (or was it his head?) with renewed force. The girl's name came to him again. He remembered exactly what she was called, this bare-footed fairy in the negligee.

'Nastya! Nastya!' Sashok exclaimed.

'What about Nastya? I've been called Nastya for – it doesn't matter how many, but for many years. It's old news.... Anything else?'

'Tell me ...what the hell was I drinking?'

'You began with Tequila. Then there was some rubbish called something like 'Hubble-Bubble'.... I remember because it sounded like 'bablo', which means 'money' in our new Russian lingo. And then a 'Hookah.''

'What on earth's that?

'But it was you who taught me! You said 'your Margaritas and Black Russians are yesterday's drinks. In England now we drink 'Hubble-Bubble'.... You called me a peasant, among other things for refusing one.'

This piece of information plunged Sashok deep into thought. He had no idea what the hell a 'Hubble-Bubble' was.... His memory was not functioning well at all.

'Listen, Nastya ... what else happened at night? I mean, apart from the booze. I have this vague memory....'

'Well, I hope you haven't forgotten the most important bits.'

'I think I have....'

'Ah, so you can't recall what happened and you're afraid you did something awful?' Nastya said, roaring with laughter and flashing her stunning white teeth. But Sashok was not in the mood for mirth.

He tried his best to remember. Wild images and forms flashed before his eyes, an oddly shaped room, the semi-darkness, naked people (he wasn't sure if they were men or women) protruding body parts (which were ugly and not at all attractive) as well as some creature of indeterminate gender dressed from head to foot in a kind of black leather and wielding a whip. For some reason Sashok spoke to him or her, saying 'What are you after?' And the freak just cracked the whip threateningly by way of a reply. Sashok could not understand if this was just a snippet from a drunken nightmare or.... The strain of it all made Sashok feel ill again and he groaned quietly.

'I would advise you to be more careful about what and how much you drink,' said Nastya.

Sashok lifted his unresponsive body and supported himself on a cushion. Now he was in a half-sitting position. But every movement he made was a tremendous effort.

'But I really did do something wrong didn't I?'

'For starters you turned out to be a racist.'

'A racist?' In what sense?'

'In the most basic sense.'

And Nastya laughed again in her infectious way.

'You mean....I....There was a black girl there, wasn't there?'

In reply Nastya nodded gleefully: there most certainly was a black girl there, without the shadow of a doubt.

'And... did I do something to upset her?'

'Yes you did and you made a pretty good job of it.' Nastya was obviously enjoying the conversation.

'And ... how did I offend her?'

'You mean you really don't remember?'

'I swear to you ... absolutely ... did I reject her advances?'

'It's much worse than that.'

'My God! What exactly did I do, then?'

Nastya got up from her armchair, came and sat on the bed, putting her arms around Sashok's shoulders. Then she whispered into his ear.

Sashok recoiled, pushed Nastya away and said in a hoarse voice,

'No. No ... impossible. I'm not capable of such a thing!'

'Oh, come on, you were drunk.... Smashed out of your mind.'

Nothing was said for a couple of minutes. Sashok just sat on his bed in a state of shock, depressed, ill and with eyes as red as a rabbit's, and Nastya turned towards the window as if she was too embarrassed to look at him. Then she stood up, yawned and stretched seductively. Her negligee rippled like a pink wave as she walked over to the window and stood there for a few seconds. Looking at her from behind was even more exciting: her amazing back and everything else seemed even more beautiful and mysterious under her nightie. But Sashok found it impossible to concentrate on this enchanting vision: the unbelievable news had come as such a shock to him.

'No,' he thought, 'there's something not right here. Someone who's drunk can behave in an unbelievably stupid way, he can be a crude caricature ... but of himself, not somebody else! What is it they say? 'What a sober man thinks a drunken man says!' But I never thought of anything like that.... Never ... and never could!'

Meantime Anastasia returned to the armchair, rummaged about a little in her handbag and took something from it. Then she asked,

'Would you like some grapes?

'Grapes? Are you joking? I fancy some pickling brine or at the very least a cup of strong coffee.'

'The first thing you need to do is drink some water otherwise you might end up being dehydrated.'

And Nastya brought out a bottle of Evian together with the carton of red grapes.

'There you go. Drink.'

Sashok, with difficulty, got up onto his knees and reached out for the bottle...

Quick as a flash Nastya hid the mineral water behind her back. Then she said,

'And do you know you also insulted *Absolument*?'

'What? Him, too?'

'Yes, and the man was upset. He even burst into tears. Cried his eyes out '

'No! I don't believe it! He actually started crying?'

'Yes.... Well, almost. Did a lot of whining aloud. It turns out he's a fragile character. Vulnerable.'

'*Absolument* ... vulnerable? I never would have thought it.... Don't tell me, I will never believe it. Surely, I didn't do to him ... the same thing like I did to Melanie?'

'No, no, calm down. You were exhausted and you were drunk.'

'So how did I offend him, then?'

'Well.... First he ... and then you....'

Nastya gesticulated in a strange way but Sashok could not figure out what she was trying to say.'

'Me? What about me?'

'You scorned him.... You really did show your contempt for *Absolument*.'

'My contempt? In what way?'

'Well, you refused.'

'How do you mean, I refused? Just a minute, you are not saying he made a pass at me?'

'Of course he did! And you refused. You said, 'What's this? I don't want any of that!''

'Did I say that to his face? In such a rude way?'

'Yes. You refused him point blank. You said you wanted none of it.'

'And what language was all this in?'

'What language? English, of course.'

'And you.....are you sure you understood?'

'Well ... I might have missed some of the details but I got the general meaning all right! It was obvious what you meant and then you made everything very clear in the traditional Russian way.'

'You mean I swore at him? *Ya rugalsya matom*?'

'You certainly did. You told him to bugger off. 'Idi na khuiy', you said. What is the English for that? Go fuck yourself or something? No, they don't know how to swear properly, those foreigners.'

'I said such a thing? But I never swear. OK, OK, that's enough... Please, give me the water.'

Nastya carried on teasing him for a bit. She held the bottle of Evian in front of his nose, then offered it to him and once again hid it behind her back. Eventually he could not take it anymore and threw himself onto the bed, moaning,

'I can't play this game. I'm going to be sick.'

'All right, then, drink,' Anastasia said, getting a bit of a fright and quickly handing him the water.

Sashok began to gulp it down.

'I'm finding all this a bit difficult to take in. I mean, talking about *Absolument*.... I saw him eyeing you.'

'Well yes, he liked me. But he's a *sovmestnik*'

'What the hell does that mean?'

'Well, he likes to wear two hats. You understand?'

'Not really.... And what about Melanie?'

'Well, Melanie was offended. And you're mainly to blame... Hey! Go easy on the water! That's enough for now... We don't want you spewing your guts up or whatever expression you refined intelligentsia types call it, do we?'

'My grandfather used to say that. Where did you dig that up from?'

'I said that's enough! Stop it! Leave me a drop of water. Don't be so selfish!'

Reluctantly Sashok gave the bottle back to Nastya, then in a state of total exhaustion, crashed out on the bed. But as soon as he closed his eyes the room began to spin. A feeling in his throat warned him that he was about to throw up. With a great effort he pulled himself into a sitting position on the bed. He stared at Nastya. She was avidly, inelegantly and unattractively sucking the last drops out of the bottle. And suddenly she looked very common and not all that beautiful.

'Disgusting! You've slobbered all over this,' exclaimed Nastya, throwing the bottle away.

'Nastya,' said Sashok firmly, 'how did I get into such a state? I didn't drink all that much. And you must have drunk quite a lot yourself but you seem all right '

'Me? I'm very fit. And I've had a lot of practice.'

'Listen, I think I must have taken some other substances, not just alcohol. Am I right?'

'Well, you smoked a little.... *Absolument* sort of treated you....'

'And I didn't refuse? Can't believe it.... Listen, tell me honestly, maybe I did something worse than that? Is it possible that I ... perhaps injected myself with something?'

'No, relax; I didn't see you doing anything like that. But you rolled some joints with *Absolument*. And by the way, they stank to high heaven.'

'I must be hallucinating,' sighed Sashok. 'And come to think of it, where exactly are we? What room is this? It doesn't look like The Cornwall Hotel to me.'

'We haven't made it to The Cornwall,' said Anastasia, lowering her eyes.

'So where are we then?'

'In The Ritz.'

'What! So that's why everything looks so chic! And the high ceilings ... and the chandelier ... and look at the bed! I've never seen such a king-size.... God knows how much all this lot costs.'

'Yes. It's not cheap. I didn't have enough money. Forgive me but I had to give them your debit card.'

'You gave them my debit card!?'

'Well, yes, the one I found in your wallet.'

Sashok put his head in his hands and quietly and ever so softly groaned.

'What am I going to do? What am I going to do? What's going to happen, what's going to happen, what's going to happen?'

'Que sera sera.... There'll be cold beer. But first, you know what's good for a hang-over?'

Sashok looked through his fingers and saw Anastasia walking towards him with a rapacious smile on her lips.

'Well, where's your Lazarus now?' she said as she let her nightie slip to the floor.

CHAPTER EIGHTEEN

The stolen face

The next few days passed as in a dream. Anastasia did not get in touch. But the most important thing was that Anna-Maria neither turned up nor phoned. Most weird of all, however, was that her parents went to great lengths to show that nothing unusual was happening. Every day they went about their business and sometimes dined with Sashok in the evenings, distracting him with idle talk. It was as though they did not have (and had never had) a daughter and, for some reason or other, just happened to have a young man from Russia staying with them. Sometimes Sashok could stand it no more and, thinking 'to hell with good manners,' would ask them straight out if Anna-Maria had called. Then they would look away, embarrassed by Sashok's ill-breeding and shake their heads. And that was the signal to change the conversation to some other topic, such as how Mr Singh was getting on.

And Mr Singh was getting on OK True, he too was behaving a little oddly; he stopped goading Sashok despite the fact that his mind was not on his work, that he was often miles away and would forgot to do what he had promised and missed deadlines for delivering material and so on. He was waiting for calls from Nastya which never came. He would stay late at work on any excuse, and would then wander the streets, going into shops without any intention of buying anything, then he would travel back to Folkestone and would spend longer and longer in front of the house, unable to bring himself to go in and trying to guess whether or not Anna-Maria had returned.

He had also hesitated in front of the beige-coloured entrance to this three-storey house the very first time he went in. But that was different: on that occasion he had been a bit nervous and shy. He had caught his breath in the expectation of something unusual and remarkable.

But not this time. This time his heart was aching from loneliness and a sickening feeling of guilt, combined with resentment at the general injustice of life. The house, which had seemed so wonderful ('I'd like one like this, one day' he used to secretly admit to himself with a sigh) now aroused feelings of revulsion. In his disturbed state Sashok could not enjoy the neatly laid-out, small, exquisitely maintained front garden with a gravel border and geometric shapes in the centre. (When he first saw them he thought he had landed among freemasons!) Now of course he had the designs fully committed to memory and could have drawn them with his eyes shut. And he also knew that neither his mother-in-law nor his wife had any connections with the masons.

In any case the design had been dreamed up by an eccentric landscape gardener called Joseph. Sashok had been given the full account of how it had happened: the landscape gardener turned up at the crack of dawn and spent a long time looking thoughtfully at the front of the house. Then he closed his eyes, shook his head a bit and suddenly took a piece of paper out of a folder and began to draw, as if in a trance, at the same time whispering something to himself, as if under a spell. Joseph assured everyone that the design was in perfect harmony with the visual aspect of the house, with its obvious and not so obvious proportions, with the shape of the windows, the slope of the roof and its colour, even if not everyone might immediately see all of this. The harmony would extend to the subconscious associations aroused by the design. Sashok soon became well acquainted with this philosophy and the whole procedure because he had the great satisfaction of watching Joseph at work when he produced a garden design for the neighbours. It was not that Sashok was fully convinced of the artist's genius but there was no denying that the front garden did go very well with the house and seemed to fit it like a well-tailored suit. And it appeared that all those who stopped to admire this work of art were of the same opinion.

As far as Freemasonry was concerned, Sashok lost all interest after he spotted, in a rather run-down part of the town, a dilapidated house with a humble sign which read 'Folkestone Masonic Hall.' It looked as prosaic and ordinary as the signs saying 'Chemist' or 'Newsagent' which adorned other buildings in the neighbourhood. But then newsagents had made their impression on Sashok, in the first place with the name of their profession. They were not 'traders in the printed word' or 'newspapers sellers' or even the 'SovPress' kiosks back home: they were known by the romantic title of 'agents of the news.' Secondly, you didn't need to be a trained accountant to realise that, with kopeck (or penny)-thin margins you couldn't make a fortune out of selling newspapers and magazines, only a very modest living at best. In this business if you just wanted to make ends meet you had to slog your guts out. Not for nothing are these little shops, like any other kind of grubby, underpaid work, so often the domain of recent immigrants. Very rarely will you see a white face behind a newsagent's counter. Usually you will find Indians, Pakistanis or, less often, Chinese there. 'Why do Russians never take it up?' Sashok wondered, and then provided his own answer. Such boring, labour-intensive work with so few prospects simply does not appeal to the Russian soul. Nevertheless there were times when it seemed to Sashok that in fact he himself could possibly take such thankless job (on a temporary basis only!) just to gain his freedom and a place to live, even if it was just a couple of rooms above a little shop, as is often the case with newsagents. But on the plus side, he would not be humiliatingly dependent on others; he would not have to play the exhausting game of appearances with constant feelings of guilt hanging in the air.

These were the thoughts that overcame Sashok at difficult moments when he was standing in front of the house secretly hoping that Anna-Maria's parents were not at home and that he would be able to have a quiet, relaxing evening on his own. But all hope would vanish the moment he would see the upstairs windows, sometimes with a light shining from the bedroom or the bathroom.

This, unfortunately, was a sign that his parents-in-law were at home. John and Maggie had no relation of course to the Russian world of 'criminals-in-law' (bandits who live by the thieves' code of honour). With his in-laws, Sashok's relations may have been 'lawful' but they were not very simple. Generally, sons-in-law are not often liked by their mothers-in-law and, and they return the compliment. But in Sashok's motherland everything is simpler, more clearly understood and predictable. Everything falls into one of the few patterns: 'he' either 'hasn't got enough money', or 'doesn't appreciate how lucky he was to get our daughter', or 'he's got an inflated opinion of himself.' There are very few variations. Judging by the stories he heard from friends, in Russia it might not be easy to cope with a mother-in-law's harassment and snide remarks, but you have a chance to survive it all if you try hard and, particularly, if your father-in-law isn't too nasty. But here, in an English home, try as you might, you could never be absolutely sure when they were happy with you and when they were not. And, most importantly, even if you manage to second-guess them you still could never tell why.

At the beginning the house seemed unbelievably large to Sashok. On the ground floor was a lounge or, as it's called here, a sitting room. There was also a separate dining room, connected by a special door to the long, rectangular kitchen. He was astonished to hear that Maggie thought that it was 'rather small'. Was this another example of English humour? As it turned out, she wasn't joking. Approximately half the kitchen, where there was a small table and a couple of chairs, was called 'the breakfast room.' It did not matter that nobody ever ate breakfast in there any more or that the table and chairs had long since gone, replaced as they were by wardrobes. As far as the family was concerned the spacious accommodation was divided into two by an invisible border. 'We cook only in this half,' Maggie explained curtly when Sashok attempted gingerly to express his bewilderment. But forget the kitchen. Sashok was much more impressed by the high ceilings with their old-fashioned mouldings, the intricate crystal chandeliers and the authentic black fire-place with beige-coloured tiles on both sides, a fire-guard and tongs and other gleaming implements intended for arranging the coals. And in addition to all this there was a cellar, a sort of large basement with its own window.

Upstairs there were two bedrooms and John's study. Anna-Maria lived on the top floor, under the eaves, which had a not very high but beautifully slanting ceiling with eye-catching beams made from polished wood. She had two rooms – a sitting room and bedroom with small windows and her own (oh, yes!) toilet and wash-hand basin. All of this wealth she now shared with Sashok who, it has to be said, did not feel as though he was the master here (far from it). In addition there were frequent guests to the house; there was Aunty Liz from Brighton and Grandfather David from Edinburgh and then various other relatives. If two guests came to stay the night at the same time one slept in the large guest room on the first floor next to the 'master bedroom' and the other slept on the second floor which meant that the young couple had to vacate their own little sitting room for a while. This was also where Anna-Maria's girl friends from a former life stayed when they occasionally turned up, like her friend from Nottingham University and another from the prestigious City of London School for Girls. And it took a while for Sashok to get used to the names given to the various floors. He knew from school that what is the second floor in Russia is the first floor in England, and then the third is the second and so on and so forth. It was one thing to know all this but quite another to get used to it and avoid confusion. At first there were times when he and his parents-in-law misunderstood each other if he said 'I'm going down to the first floor' when, in their minds, he was already on the first floor. Or 'I'm going up to the third floor' when, counting the floors the English way, there was no third floor in the house at all. Sashok even thought that John and Maggie had come to the conclusion that their son-in-law was probably a bright lad but a bit absent-minded. And of course Sashok's reputation suffered from one or two other silly incidents, when he was feeling nervous and uncomfortable, and still getting to grips with a strange way of life and unfamiliar, complicated rules and customs. And, as we all know, the first impressions are the strongest and prejudices formed at first acquaintance are the most difficult to shake off. For instance, on probably the second day of living in England, Sashok put his foot in it when he was looking at the family photograph album (a most important and indispensable step in the formation of lasting bonds with one's English relatives) and made some frank remarks about Aunty Liz's size.

It took him a long time to remember that you have to put the lid of the toilet down every time after you use it. And that asking questions about the value of somebody's house or how much they earn is a mark of very poor upbringing, whereas the price of food and complaints about the cost of living are a perfectly acceptable topic of conversation, coming third (or fourth) after the weather, summer holidays and problems with public transport.

And Sashok also looked stupid when he brought his indoor slip-ons with him from Moscow. Nobody, apart from him, took his shoes off the moment he came indoors and his stubborn adherence to this Russian tradition was taken as a challenge.

But he was also guilty of other more fundamental gaffs. It took him a long time to realize that the answer to the question 'How are you?' could be only a short and simple phrase like 'I'm fine, thank you' or 'Couldn't be better' or 'Not too bad.' To complain about life in answer to the question 'How are you?' is considered extremely bad form and to go into detailed explanations about the circumstances of one's existence is a sign of intellectual inadequacy.

Now Sashok got into the habit of 'turning the pages of the book of his life with disgust', to use a famous Pushkin's quote. In vain did he try to reason with himself, pointing out that things were not all that awful after all. OK, his in-laws might have seen him as some kind of an oddball. But it shouldn't have been a catastrophe. In the first place, the English are accustomed to eccentricity of all kinds, and for them this gentleman from Russia was a source not just of irritation but of entertainment, too. In the second place, and more importantly, these were rather kind people, the living illustration of the well-known saying about the difference between the English and the French. The saying that he so nonchalantly quoted to Anastasia - about how both nations look down on foreigners; but while the French despise them, the English pity them. Still, he was feeling more and more like a loser.

There were times when Sashok hated the very idea of going into the house and having to speak to John and Maggie so much that he even thought of hiding in the garden till night time: there were plenty of good places for it. The Mannings' garden would have been considered pretty large in Russia, but by British standards it was fairly average. From the occasional vague hint, Sashok was able to guess that his parents-in-law could easily have afforded to buy themselves a slightly larger house in a more prestigious area, especially when John was at the peak of his career as a big shot in the City. Exactly how big Sashok was not quite sure as his attempts to find out all about his father-in-law's career always met stiff opposition. John was somewhat self-effacing and insisted he was just a small cog in an enormous financial wheel. Whatever the case, the Mannings had become attached to the house which they had acquired through hard work during their poverty-stricken younger days. This was quite a common phenomenon among the middle classes and even among the so-called 'upper-middle class' types. And for some reason they were also extremely fond of the town. 'They'll carry me out of Folkestone in a box,' John would sometimes say. 'And most of all I like my garden,' Maggie would add with heartfelt sincerity.

And there is no doubt that the garden was beautiful and well cared-for. Its biggest and furthest part, up against the neighbours' wall, combined a lawn, a rose bed, and vivid orange bushes which provided a lateral framework for the garden (Sashok could never remember what on earth they were called). There was also a 'shed,' a pretty little construction where all kinds of garden implements were stored and where Sashok and Anna-Maria had set up a little improvised sitting-room with two deck-chairs and a tiny little table. They would sometimes seek refuge here 'for a smoke,' which usually meant that they just wanted to get away from John, Maggie and their guests and spend some time together. And right next to the house was the part of the garden which was separated from the rest by a hedge, a sort of patio with a large, green metal table and chairs, where the family would enjoy Sunday lunch when the weather was fine.

Sashok's mother, the one and only time she decided to visit the British Isles, took a liking to the garden. 'You've got a town flat with its own *dacha*', she said. In reply Sashok just mumbled something indistinct and nodded in vague agreement. There was nothing else he could do: he did not like gardens and did not understand what they were about: he was still not old enough. Nor did he like to see John and Maggie labouring with such religious fervour in the garden: the spectacle was not for the faint-hearted. Shouldn't we feel sorry for people who, after working hard all week, slave away and allow themselves no rest on their day-off? And then it seemed to Sashok that their every gesture, facial expression together with the things they said to him was a constant rebuke. Why was it that he, a fit, strapping thirty-odd-year-old, did not come running to help his parents-in-law?

He never came to their aid for the simple reason that he hated this kind of work and considered it a complete waste of time. Well OK, he could have kept his opinions to himself and put up with doing a bit of work for the sake of family harmony. But his real problem was that he was, as they say in English, 'all fingers and thumbs.' The Russians, by the way, also have a graphic expression: 'my hands are hooks' and when Sashok translated this wonderful idiom for Anna-Maria she was not impressed and replied 'why hooks?' Oh, what else would you expect from an English woman? Sashok despaired.

But the principal problem was not a linguistic one. It was the fact that a lack of skill in, or love for, gardening was seen in the family as a serious personal defect. Of course this opinion was never voiced aloud, but Sashok sensed it was there deep down.

But all this was his former existence, an existence with its minor tribulations and small joys. Now an unexpectedly sharp about-turn was under way.

These days Sashok would enter the house with a sigh and would be met with something bordering on polite hostility. With difficulty he would sit out the tedious evenings and seek refuge in the bedroom as soon as possible and on the slightest pretext. It is true that his wife's parents did, from time to time, attempt to relieve the tension by suggesting that they could watch together a football match or a charity concert in Hyde Park. His parents-in-law moved Sashok deeply when they remembered the anniversary of his arrival in England, the anniversary that he had forgotten all about. On the floor by the door into his room he found not only a postcard with a view of Dover but a parcel tied up with a pink ribbon. Picking it up he immediately guessed what was inside: another brief-case, just like the one he had lost. Then he could not get to sleep but tossed and turned and carried on an imaginary argument with Anna-Maria and then with Nastya. One night he dreamed that the women had got to know each other and were together giving him a hard time, scolding him hard. Towards morning he slid into oblivion and then, when the alarm went off, he opened his eyes with great difficulty and made his way unsteadily to the bathroom.

One day the inevitable happened: it was a Thursday and Sashok did not hear the alarm clock and overslept. He woke up just after nine. He telephoned Mr Singh in the office, told him some nonsense about engineering works on the line (how easily, it turned out, he had learned to lie!) and looking half-mad, with his hair unkempt, sprinted to the station.

Folkestone Central looked different from what it was at seven. And the difference was in the people; he was now surrounded by new, unfamiliar commuters. Most of them were pensioners, others looked slightly bohemian. There were also a remarkable number of aging French people. Then Sashok spotted the only person he recognised....Harry! And he was as pleased to see him as if he were one of his own.

Harry was drinking tea in the station buffet, where Sashok usually never even set foot as it was so smoky. He waved both hands at Sashok enthusiastically as he was standing hesitantly in the doorway.

Sashok took one step into the buffet and just had time to exchange a few words with Harry when he heard the noise of the approaching train behind him. He turned round, stepped back onto the platform and ....

There was Anna-Maria getting into the carriage nearest the exit. But she was not alone. She was with a young man sporting the blue tweed jacket, precisely like the one that Sashok was so fond of. And the trousers the man was wearing, made of fine woollen grey material, were similar to those that Sashok usually put on with the tweed jacket. The stranger's black shoes with metal fastenings also looked familiar. In fact, everything he was wearing looked like the clothes Sashok often wore. And when the young man turned in the direction of the platform in order to close the steel door Sashok saw a familiar face, too – his own.

CHAPTER NINETEEN

A terrifying explanation

On that unforgettable morning on the platform of Folkestone Central station Sashok, for the first time in his life, discovered the exact meaning of the Russian expression 'vatnye nogi', 'cotton legs' or 'jelly legs', as the English might say. This discovery occurred precisely at the moment when he saw himself getting onto the train with Anna-Maria. His legs may or may not have been made out of cotton or jelly but they did appear to lose their fundamental purpose and were not willing to support Sashok in a vertical position any more. His head began to spin and he sensed a terrifying feeling of emptiness in his stomach and chest. Sashok was even forced to grab hold of the open door of the buffet to avoid falling over. Meanwhile, the train had moved off and the silhouettes of Anna-Maria and her unbelievable companion, now settled into their seats, flashed past. Sashok felt an urgent need for the toilet. Getting there (a distance of 15-20 feet) turned out to be not at all easy but, fine fellow that he was, he managed it.

After his visit to this establishment Sashok felt a bit better. But now he had to face torments which were more of the mind. Sashok was desperate to find an answer, some sort of working hypothesis which might explain what had happened. The most obvious explanation did not appeal to him; after all, who wants to admit to mental disorder? He was keen to hear some alternative suggestions.

Sashok decided that the first thing he should do will be to sit down for a few minutes in the station buffet and have a cup of tea, while trying to collect his thoughts. But no sooner had he stepped inside than he spotted Harry the burglar who, for some reason, had not gone anywhere but was sitting quietly at a table, sipping coffee and smoking a cigarette. Sashok's first impulse was to turn and run, but, as soon as he saw Sashok, Harry came to life and began waving his arms about in a beckoning gesture. Sashok could not bring himself to turn and leave. 'I'll cadge a fag off him,' he thought. Then his inner voice chipped in: 'you really have gone mad; you haven't smoked for nearly eleven years.' 'So what?' growled Sashok, 'I need something to steady my nerves.' 'You might be better off with a slug of vodka.' his inner voice answered, meekly. 'It may come to that, too,' replied Sashok, as he walked towards Harry who had happily jumped up to meet him. A few seconds later Sashok was also sitting at the table and Harry, as if he was able to read his thoughts, offered him a cigarette. Then a plastic cup of steaming hot tea materialised out of nowhere and Harry, winking in an almost conspiratorial manner, took a silver flask out of an inside pocket and, without saying a word, added a healthy dash of Irish whiskey to Sashok's tea. When he had taken a sip of the hot strong tea, laced with the 40° proof Jameson's, followed by long drag on his cigarette, Sashok felt his head spinning again, but this time the sensation was so much more pleasant. 'Just what I needed,' he thought. Take a hit, give a hit.

'What's the matter sir?' asked Harry, looking anxiously into Sashok's face. 'I have to say, I've never seen you looking so.......distraught before. Do you feel well?'

Sashok was unable to speak and just wrung his hands.

'I think your brother is around, isn't he? Has he come to visit? I think I just saw him getting on the train with Anna-Maria. An amazing likeness!' said Harry. He probably thought it would do good to engage Sashok in a light-hearted chat about the family, but he may have regretted this kind intention as Sashok suddenly shouted out, so that the whole buffet could hear, and Harry nearly choked on his tea.

'I haven't got a frigging brother!'

'But hold on a minute, I distinctly saw....' said Harry before falling silent with embarrassment.

Sashok took a swig of the steaming potion, calmed down a bit and said,

'What exactly did you see, Harry? A man who looked remarkably like me? Two peas in a pod, eh? But if that's the case, why did you shut up in embarrassment? Bit awkward to ask, is it? Well, come on then, let's play by Russian rules. For us it's perfectly normal to ask questions about anything unusual if it arouses natural curiosity. Or aren't you curious?'

'I certainly am!' said Harry, cheering up a bit. 'So do tell me, Mr Tutov, who was that young man who looked so much like you? And why the hell was he going off somewhere on the train with your wife?'

'Aha,' said Sashok, 'so it wasn't a hallucination! It means that I really did see myself.....or rather, someone who looks mysteriously like me.'

'And is, moreover, travelling with your own wife.'

'But that's another question ... was it really my wife?'

Harry again fell silent, as if stunned by the question, but then asked, nervously,

'What do you mean?'

Sashok knew he probably should have kept the improbable story to himself but he desperately needed to get it off his chest, to confide in somebody, even if it was a stranger with a dodgy reputation. And so it happened that he started spilling the beans– with a few omissions of course.

Harry was all ears and just now and again interrupted the tale with murmured interjections such as 'Oh dear!', 'You never!', 'They didn't!' and other English expressions designed for a tactful manifestation of surprise. Both sides understood the relative inadequacy of these conventional and hackneyed linguistic measures which are used as polite reactions to the normal incidents of everyday existence. These are the phrases you resort to when, let's say, you discover that the person you are talking to got up half an hour earlier than usual, or left his glasses at home or that the bin men arrived to collect the rubbish on Wednesday instead of Friday.

Nothing more surprising than this is supposed to happen to a lady or to a gentleman and if something really untoward occurs they will just not talk about it openly. The situation which Sashok was describing was quite exceptional and the fact that he was speaking so openly without equivocation or constraint was also beyond normal bounds. What was Harry supposed to do? How should he react? What words should he utter to express the fact that he appreciated Sashok's frankness and the importance of the secrets which he was entrusting to him? But alas, he couldn't find more dramatic expressions and so was obliged to resort to other, non-verbal, means of expression. He strengthened his banal exclamations by occasionally slapping Sashok on the leg, or by whistling softly, grunting and snorting. And from time to time Sashok saw doubt in Harry's eyes. 'He's not fully convinced that I am not pulling his leg,' Sashok decided.

The essence of the story boiled down to the following: one day he was offered the choice between two similar briefcases and he mistakenly chose the wrong one. Then he had to choose between his wife and a woman who looked like her lost twin and again he.... well, he sort of made another mistake. And now he was facing something even more bizarre, and at the same time frightening, calling into question his own identity. Is there a double of himself who leads life of his own in parallel to Sashok's?

'Sounds like total nonsense, doesn't it? ' Sashok asked when he finished his fevered tale.

'Mm...' murmured Harry in reply, 'it's certainly an unusual story, but let's not exaggerate or get too excited.'

'But how ... how would you explain all this?' yelled Sashok giving the girl behind the counter yet another fright.

'Calm down, calm down a bit.... Don't shout,' said Harry. 'You know what? All this sounds to me like an elaborate prank. Perhaps some drama students are practising in their holidays.'

'But of course! Why did I not think of that? Yes! That would explain everything!'

Sashok suddenly felt greatly relieved. Well done, Harry, thank you! It did not matter who he really was – a burglar, an insurance agent or simply a kind-hearted regular guy. That's common sense for you. How stupid that Sashok didn't want to confide in him only a few moments ago.

That was indeed who they were: students from a drama faculty, perhaps from the Shepkinskiy school. Or maybe from the Moscow Art Theatre studio school. Now everything was falling into place. Let's suppose that they had been invited to Britain as exchange students and on the way they decided to have a bit of fun with some set piece about the Russian mafia and their fellow-countrymen abroad. Sashok imagined the students getting together after a 'performance' and how the oldest among them, Byenik, would boast 'I think we duped him all right! Imagine, he even believed that a Russian could be called Byenik!' And the black man Dynkin would roar with laughter, flashing his white teeth and slapping Lyosha on the back. 'I don't know how I managed not to burst out laughing and keep a straight face!' And Anastasia, covering her eyes, would say 'I don't know about you guys, but I do feel sorry for him.... He might be a bit naïve, but there's something about him.... he's nice, like a kitten.' 'No,' interrupts the Gentleman, their older mentor, haughtily, 'we should have found someone else; it was too easy dealing with this credulous character ....' 'Don't forget,' says Byenik firmly, 'we chose him because....'

'Indeed, why me?' thought Sashok and said to Harry,

'One thing I still don't understand is why they picked me for their training project.'

'Oh, yes,' said Harry, 'that is the question that has been bothering me a bit, too. Of course, it is possible that they spotted you purely by chance as one of the girl students bore a remarkable resemblance to your wife. If this is the case, then it's easy to see how it gave them the idea in the first place.'

'Sounds logical,' Sashok agreed.

'Yes, but, taking a couple of special circumstances into account ... It would be a good idea to double check ... to make sure that it isn't....'

'What?' said Sashok, surprised. 'What circumstances exactly? What do you want to double check? I don't understand.'

For some reason Harry didn't look Sashok in the eye. He began to shuffle about on his chair. Then he tried to change the subject in a particularly clumsy manner.

But Sashok would not let him.

'No, no, Harry. We Russians say 'You can't say 'A' and not say 'B'.'

'Well, I just want to eliminate some other possible explanations for what happened to you.'

'For instance?'

'In your country I understand that there's a powerful organisation called the KGB.'

'Nowadays it's got another name.'

'That doesn't matter, does it? Whatever it's called it's got a special department called 'S' branch. Have you heard of it?'

'Yes, I read something about it in the magazine Top Secret. But I'm astonished, Harry. How do you know about it?'

'Do you think I don't read newspapers and magazines? I also love books about this kind of thing. I've got books by Gordeivskiy, Suvorov, Mitrokhin, not to mention John Barron.'

'I've never heard of half these names....'

'You should have, my friend, you should have. In a nutshell, Department S, Mister Tutov, deals with the so called 'illegal espionage'; they plant sleepers into Western countries....'

'Now when you tell me I recollect that I heard about it.... Yes, Gavrilov (he's a friend of mine; we were in the same class) told me something about it. His father was involved in some way with them, but to be honest, I didn't ask too many questions.'

'Department S, Mister Tutov, is concerned with infiltrating super-agents into western countries. But first they create a cover story. They take the biography from real people of a suitable age but who have died. And there also has to be a physical resemblance. Then they are infiltrated in pairs - man and wife.'

'So the man has to resemble somebody....'

'Yes, and then they choose a wife for him.... Ideally she has to look like the wife of the original. Or, on the other hand, they might choose a 'wife' and then look for a 'husband.'

'And they don't mind? They get married on the orders of their bosses?'

'Oh, you don't understand, Mr Tutov. These are not ordinary people and normal human emotions don't exist for them. It can take up to ten years to prepare them and turn them into complete zombies: something between robots and super-men.'

Sashok sat mechanically finishing his cold tea. His cigarette was burning down between his fingers as he absorbed the information. In a long and angered gest Sashok put out the remains of the cigarette in the ashtray. Then he said:

'But what if the original couples are still alive?'

'Well, they have ways of correcting such an eventuality.'

It suddenly seemed to Sashok as though all the air had been sucked out of his lungs and there was nothing left for him to breathe.

CHAPTER TWENTY

Sashok gets himself a spook - and more

Harry was beaming, very pleased with the shattering effect his new theory had had on Sashok.

'There you go, mate', he said. 'It shouldn't have been such a surprise to you. Those iron men in your Cheka, in your KGB, they were truly dreadful people: Felix Dzerzhinsky, Pavel Sudoplatov and General Vlasik, surely, these names you have heard!'

But when he saw that Sashok was completely deflated, he took pity on him and clapped him on the shoulder offering words of consolation,

'Now don't you go thinking that this is the only theory, Alexander, there are other possibilities, too.'

'I hope the others aren't so terrifying.'

Harry hesitated, and the painful process of thinking was written all over his round face. Then, in embarrassment and without looking at Sashok he said,

'To be honest, I don't really know....'

'That doesn't sound very reassuring,' Sashok observed gloomily.

'Never mind, never mind... I'll pour you another drop of Irish.....'

And he was true to his word. Harry did pour Sashok an un-Englishly generous slug, so that in the end Sashok got the feeling he was drinking not tea with whiskey but rather whiskey with tea! And the result was soon evident.

'Harry,' Sashok said, beginning to slur his words slightly, 'I am grateful to Fate that at this moment in time, at this very unfortunate time ... you are at my side.'

Then he hiccupped and, to his own surprise added,

'People here say all sorts of things about you, but I don't believe....'

'What exactly do people say about me?' asked Harry cautiously. 'I'd be very interested to know, please continue.'

Now it was Sashok's turn to feel embarrassed.

'No, I didn't mean.... Why should I repeat such rubbish.'

'Come on, do me a favour ... how does the saying go? If you say B, say the BBC.'

'I'm not going to tell you,' said Sashok stubbornly, pursing his lips and sitting up straight. 'So don't ask me.'

'Couldn't you give me a clue, at least' Harry went on as he unexpectedly poured Sashok yet another little drop from his wonderful flask. 'After all, nobody else is going to tell me. I'm relying on you.'

Sashok thought for a moment, took a sip from his cardboard cup and said:

'Well, OK ... considering ... only you won't be offended, will you?'

'I promise,' Harry solemnly declared and even half covered his eyes with his palm to show that he was ready to hear the truth, however bitter it turned out to be.

'OK,' Sashok made up his mind. 'They say that you....But, mind you, I don't believe them, not in the least, especially now that you and I have got to know each other a bit better.... No, I can't. Such nonsense!'

'Don't be afraid ... tell me what this nonsense is.'

'I can't! I can't get my tongue around it,'

'Just go for it! I'm telling you, I won't be upset. Quite the contrary....'

'OK, OK Since you insist.... Around town they say that you ... that you're a ... burglar, and that you rob houses and flats!'

Harry seemed somewhat disappointed by this information.

'Oh, that,' he said, yawning. 'And here was I thinking....'

After a brief pause he said,

'I don't give a damn about that. I'd rather you told me more about the girl who looks so much like your wife. What did you say her name was?'

'Nastya....' said Sashok suddenly with a sigh.

Harry asked in surprise:

'What? What kind of name is that?'

'Believe me, in Russian it sounds beautiful. Oh, so very beautiful! You probably can't understand that. It's a diminutive form of the name Anastasia, it's a kind of term of endearment.'

Sashok, evidently, pronounced the word 'endearment' in such an affectionate way that Harry gave him a suspicious sideways glance and frowned in consternation. Then he demanded,

'Right. Now give me the full details.'

Sashok was on the point of blurting out, 'I don't want to talk about her!' But at the last moment he remembered that he had practically just accused the man of being a thief and a rogue (although perhaps not in those exact words) and in so doing had been terribly rude to him. According to local custom it would now be appropriate to equal the score by making some shameful confession of his own.

And Sashok could contain himself no longer. With some perverse enjoyment he began to recount all the details of his affair with Nastya.

'Yes, I know,' he said, 'it was a beastly thing for me to do, to go and cheat on my wonderful, kind, intelligent, beautiful wife. But, good God, Nastya is such a tremendous lover! Unforgettable! There are no words to describe what I experienced. I think every woman-chaser in the world will be jealous of me!'

Harry looked at Sashok with a hint of pity and said:

'So what now then? Are you going to keep up the relationship with her?'

'I don't know.... I mean I know that I've got to beg Anna-Maria for forgiveness, fall at her feet. But I must be honest. If I saw Nastya standing in front of me now ... if I looked into her eyes again ... and if she wanted me ... I am not sure whether I wouldn't then....'

'I don't think you will see her again. At least not in the foreseeable future,' Harry suddenly interrupted Sashok's outpourings. 'She's gone away with this ... with the other.'

And Harry made a strange descriptive gesture with both hands as if he was having trouble finding a word to describe Nastya's travelling companion.

'This other man who ... looks so much like me' Sashok said morosely.

The recollection of the surrealistic scene on the platform began to sober Sashok up and he asked:

'Harry, aren't you going to pour me another drop of your poison?'

'Sorry, but no,' replied Harry. 'Aren't you on your way to work? So go on then. The London train will be here in five minutes. I can tell you from experience that, at moments like these, work is a great antidote against unpleasant thoughts. And you mustn't let anything disturb your normal routine, it could be your salvation.'

'Normal routine indeed,' muttered Sashok darkly.

But Harry surprised him again when he suddenly said,

'You know what? I've got a suggestion for you. I'm ... how should I put it?... a kind of private detective, in addition to my other professions, and as things are a bit slack at the moment ... I could do with a bit of practice, you might say. So, if you were to decide ... I could offer you my services.'

'How do you mean?' said Sashok.

'Well I could, let's say, observe what is going on at the Cornwall Hotel, for example.'

'What? You're offering to spy on Nastya? How could you even think of it?'

'Look, I am making the offer and it's up to you whether you want to take it. Goodbye and have a nice day, Mister Tutov.'

Harry clearly felt offended. He stood up and made his way to the door of the buffet. But he had not gone far when Sashok called after him,

'Please, Harry, come back. I'm sorry but as you know I've got good reason not to be myself today. Of course, I would be very grateful if you could....'

'You want me to do a little spying for you after all?'

'Well, if that's what you call it. But I want you to observe not just Nastya but that man as well. In fact, follow him first!'

At this point Sashok tried to copy the strange gesture which Harry had used to describe Nastya's companion.

'Understood,' said Harry. 'Let's get on the train and on the way you can tell me how to find the Cornwall hotel.'

'But I don't have any money,' Sashok suddenly remembered. 'How can I pay you for your services?'

'I'll do you a special deal: I'll work for two days for nothing as a kind of promotion special offer,' Harry said, seriously. 'And for the next two days I will give you a twenty percent discount. And if need be, you can have up to six months interest-free credit. You can manage that!'

'But what if the work takes more than four days?'

'It won't take more than four days. In four days time I'm off on my holidays, I'm going to Madeira.... Have you ever been there?'

'No, but I've heard it's very nice.'

'That's not the word for it. Climate is fantastic but the main thing is that there's practically no crime there. People don't even bother to lock their doors. Can you imagine that?'

Nothing special happened during the journey and by the time they got to Tonbridge Sashok was completely sober again. And with sobriety came terrible feeling of shame for having bared his soul to Harry about Nastya. Sashok chattered loudly away nonstop as he tried to smother his embarrassment now and again remembering that he should really be speaking in a whisper. Harry appeared to be the most grateful listener on earth as he avidly soaked up every morsel of information about the saga. Over and over again he asked Sashok to repeat certain episodes and did not tire of saying, at the appropriate moments, 'You don't say!' 'Really?' etc. True, there were a few times when he asked Sashok rather strange questions such as whether or not Anna-Maria and her parents ever discussed what was happening on the stock market; whether her father had contacts in the City (to which Sashok replied 'Of course! What self-respecting British family doesn't follow the FTSE or doesn't have friends in the City?'). Harry was obviously considering how to frame the next question, when the guard announced in his hoarse voice 'London Bridge.' Sashok just had time to jump off the train onto the painfully familiar platform, waving 'good-bye' to Harry and saying 'See you.' The train moved off and Sashok saw Harry at the carriage window with the question still frozen on his lips. 'Off he goes to do his spying,' thought Sashok and he didn't feel good about it. 'I should not have agreed to this venture,' he thought dejectedly as he walked across London Bridge, totally oblivious to his surroundings. Then he had a mental picture of the man who had given him such a shock....he remembered the dreadful feeling he experienced when he seemed to be looking at himself. 'Well, yes,' his inner voice said, 'gives you a worse kick in the balls than any number of Red Bulls.' And he experienced yet another shock when he realised that the man's travelling companion was Anna-Maria or Nastya. At this point his little voice whined, 'Come on! You knew immediately it was Nastya, don't pretend otherwise.'

Who were those people? Could they really be super-agents who wanted to take the place of Sashok and his wife in real life? What a cheek! After all, he and Anna-Maria had hardly begun their life together the way they should have done; they still had everything to look forward to and it was not too late for everything to turn out OK. Why did someone have the right to snatch their future from them in the name of some stupid espionage purposes? Or perhaps they didn't and all this was a kind of nonsense; nowadays things like this only happen in the movies. So who are they then, these people: actors, bandits or aliens from another planet?

'Anything is possible' was the gloomy summing up of the situation offered by Sashok's inner voice, which then added, 'Pack up all these thoughts. We have arrived.'

And indeed Sashok found himself standing in front of the entrance to Century Building. This was the last place on earth he wanted to be and the last person on earth he wanted to see was Mr Singh, as he would have to make abject apologies to him. What a humiliation! 'No, I'm not going to apologise. I'll just walk through to my desk as if nothing had happened and the merciless Indian can sack me or whatever! And all kind of inner voices can go and hang themselves or whatever they do when their advice is ignored' ' Sashok decided.

He was expecting an ugly scene, but there was nothing of the kind. True, when he first walked into the office there was a strange kind of silence in the air, and everybody avoided eye-contact ('They know something,' his inner voice gave its pennyworth, 'To hell with them!' Sashok answered with pride.) He walked calmly past Mr Singh's little office, saw some kind of movement there out of the corner of his eye, and nodded back. Then he sat down at his desk. He placed his briefcase on it and then, not believing his ears, heard his own rather laid-back voice saying:

'Dear colleagues, why don't I see happiness on your faces at the sight of a comrade who is restored to health? Surely you missed me?'

Then the miracle happened. The first to react was Tsveta, the Bulgarian girl. She ran to Sashok and kissed him three times, once on one cheek, then once on the other and then again, apparently accidentally, partially on the lips. She had never done anything like this before! At this point Vugar came up to him slowly, shook him warmly by the hand and whispered in his ear,

'Well done! I am so glad!'

Then Lee, the Russian of Korean extraction, sidled up and, smiling from ear to ear said in a lowered voice,

'Astonishing news. We're all ecstatic!'

'Indeed,' answered Sashok and, not quite knowing what he was agreeing with, added, 'of course.'

He tried not to look astounded, but in reality he was getting closer and closer to a state of panic: what the hell was going on? Another prank or practical joke? In no time at all a circle had formed around his desk. Everyone was smiling, someone was quietly giggling and somebody else shook his hand as if to congratulate him about something. Then the circle dispersed and Mr Singh's magnificent turban appeared. 'If he hurls himself at me and starts kissing me then I really am dreaming,' thought Sashok who by now was ready for anything. But Mr Singh did not kiss him, but instead announced imperiously,

'Mister Tutov, allow me to introduce to you the director of the Tiraspol textile company, our principal client in Moldova.' Sashok stood up and shook hands with a stocky, middle-aged man. 'This is Mister Lupanu,' said Mr Singh, continuing the introductions, 'and this is Mr Tutov, our new owner. He has only just (today, to be precise) bought Century Building Publishers Ltd.'

Lupanu took Sashok's hand in an earnest, vice-like grip and began to shake it vigorously. He was so choked with emotion that he could not utter a word. Sashok was also speechless. So they just stood there for a few moments, shaking each other by the hand like two deaf and slightly deranged mutes while their colleagues stood around them observing the scene with increasing astonishment.

CHAPTER TWENTY ONE

A rich woman's husband

From the direction of the White Cliffs of Dover there was still no sound to indicate the arrival of an approaching train and Sashok was sitting on a bench, with his briefcase on his left-hand side. It was one of those rare occasions when, after being late the previous day, he had arrived early at the station. Now he was feeling at a loose end, sitting miserably all alone, struggling with his disturbing thoughts. He was miles away and failed to notice the person who suddenly sat down next to him on the bench. Sashok turned and saw a rather unattractive man in a white raincoat wearing a cap and dark glasses. With obvious effort, coughing and wheezing, the stranger settled himself on the bench and placed his own briefcase close to his side. Sashok was about to move away a bit from this character and put him out of his mind, but then he suddenly noticed something which made him gasp for breath. His eyes didn't want to believe what they were seeing but there was no room for doubt: again two identical briefcases were standing side by side, like twin brothers. Sashok became alarmed and immediately made up his mind to let the stranger know that the game was up. For starters Sashok uttered an indistinct sound, a bit like 'Mmmm … eh'. His neighbour did not react. 'Eeeh … eeh' said Sashok, this time a little louder. Zero attention. 'Perhaps he doesn't understand English,' he thought.

'Listen, I....' Sashok started a little nervously in Russian, but the stranger was in no mind to listen to what Sashok had to say.

He just placed his hand on Sashok's new briefcase – the one only recently given to him as a present by his in-laws.

'Excuse me!' Sashok cried out, this time at the top of his voice. The stranger took no notice. He sat there for a few seconds, gently moaning under his breath and then muttered rather indistinctly, 'oh, it's so-oh rotten!'

All the while his hand remained on Sashok's property. The character then hiccupped and said,

'We shouldn't have topped it up with liquor. Cointreau it's called. Real shit!'

Then a warm, dark wave enveloped Sashok. *Pyeregar* was the half-forgotten Russian word which came to his mind. It conjured up stale, booze-laden breath the morning after. But this particular *pyeregar* was no ordinary one – it was so exceptional that it made Sashok's head spin a little. Until now he had never suspected that such a powerful wave of gaseous alcohol made worse by some dreadful aromatic additives could emanate from a human mouth. The man stood up, swayed a little, picked up the briefcase and set off with it, unsteadily, to the station exit. 'No! Not again!' shouted Sashok, setting off in pursuit. But, as ever, he was unlucky. It just happened that at that precise moment a Chinaman and a whole litter of children came out of the buffet and Sashok lost a few precious seconds as he attempted to skirt around them. The white raincoat flashed briefly at the top of the ramp down from the platform and the man seemed to turn round and wave to Sashok as if to say 'Keep cool, man, it's all under control'. Sashok, muttering 'Excuse me, excuse me,' tore through the Chinese multitude, but then he was stopped by two further incidents. And it was utterly impossible not to react to them.

In the first place the train rolled in. But – wonder of wonders! – it was not the usual rickety museum piece. No, it consisted of spanking new white carriages with enormous tinted glass windows and jolly, yellow doors. Sashok would not have been more astonished had the Flying Dutchman sailed up to the platform on Folkestone Central. The train was so unbearably beautiful that Sashok froze for a couple of seconds, spell-bound by the vision. 'But of course! They've been promising us new French carriages but nobody really believed it....

And here they are!' thought Sashok just as someone standing behind him quietly said, 'Alexander....'

And this was the second incident: Harry had reappeared. He was not immediately recognisable as he was disguised by a grey bomber-jacket and a cap which was pulled down low over his eyes.

'Harry, they've swapped briefcases with me again!' exclaimed Sashok.

'Impossible,' Harry replied, frowning. 'On the other hand, with these characters everything is possible. Where's the one they left?

Sashok nodded in the direction of the bench where the twin to Sashok's now lost briefcase stood in lonely splendour. Harry ran up to the platform attendant and whispered something in his ear. ('He's asking him to hold the train,' thought Sashok). Then he moved very cautiously towards the briefcase and did something very odd with it. It seemed to Sashok that Harry pressed the briefcase for a second or two between his elbows, rocked it very gently, put it to his ear and moved his hand over it carefully. Then he took a pair of thick gloves out of his pocket, put them on and then picked the briefcase up, very gently, as one would lift a small child. All this took just a few seconds. Then Harry turned to Sashok and said,

'Get on the train. We've got to get to London, fast!'

He nodded to the guard and said 'Cheers, mate.' Then he grabbed Sashok, who was still in a kind of daze, by the arm and dragged him onto the train. At that moment the doors closed with a soft swishing sound.

Harry towed Sashok to the far end of the carriage where no other passengers were sitting, sat down at one of the little tables and covered it with a kind of oil-cloth which he pulled out of the cavernous interior of his coat pocket. Then he produced a magnifying glass and began to examine the handle of the unfamiliar briefcase.

'No, it's definitely not a bomb,' he said, 'they're not that stupid.... I'm more worried that there might be some sort of tiny poisoned spike hidden in the handle or they might just have smeared it with ricin.... but I can't see anything like that. Nevertheless, it's a bit early to relax; I want to have a look inside.'

Sashok, with eyes like dinner plates and his mouth wide open, sat opposite Harry and watched as he worked his magic on the briefcase. He prodded the lock with something (it looked like a thin piece of plastic) and then there was click and the case opened.

'Careful!' said Harry 'You'd better sit a bit further away.'

'No way,' said Sashok, valiantly deciding that he was not going to give in to his fear.

'Now!' ordered Harry. 'Move three rows down the carriage.'

Unwillingly, Sashok gave in. A few agonising moments passed. The train had already stopped at Sandling station when Harry addressed Sashok in his normal, polite, almost servile tones, with all the imperious notes gone from his voice,

'Mister Tutov, please, have a look in here. Nothing dangerous ... just a few strange objects.'

The objects spread out on the oil-cloth were indeed strange and painfully familiar: a rusty alarm clock, a ball of string, a woman's trainer (for the right, not the left, foot); playing cards (just the coloured ones); a copy of the 'Morning Star' from 1987.

'But where's the 'Luso-Japanese Ecological Dictionary?' muttered Sashok.

'What dictionary?' Harry sounded surprised.

'Luso. Luso-Japanese. But logically it really should be Japanese-Luso.'

'Oh, I don't know anything about that,' said Harry as he peered inside the briefcase. 'I must say their methods seem to be somewhat repetitive ... quite boring actually.... No imagination.... Oh, just a minute, what is that? Look, there is something behind this zip.'

And Harry gently removed from a 'secret' compartment of the briefcase (Sashok had never used it) a small black velvet case with gold lettering.

'What's that?' Sashok asked.

'Hold on, take it easy. We have to be careful....'

Harry examined the case, twisted his mouth sceptically and said,

'Alexander, do you mean to tell me that you have never seen this object before?'

'Never.'

'So do I take it that it's not yours?'

'Of course not! And it wasn't here the last time either. No black case, no gold lettering ... nothing! There was an alarm clock, a trainer and the cards, and even the dictionary. But this case was not there. And I looked everywhere, including behind the zip ... but ... what is it?'

'This, Mr Tutov, is a certificate for half a million shares in a company called 'Ertera Group PLC.'

'Who owns them? Whose name are the shares in?' asked Sashok

'It says here: Mrs Anna-Maria Tutov,' said Harry, looking at Sashok with scarcely disguised suspicion.

'You must be kidding!'

'Kidding? Here, have a look for yourself.'

Harry handed Sashok the case and he looked inside.

'This certificate's a joke!' Sashok said. 'You get a more professional-looking one for crossing the equator on a tourist cruise!'

'Well, I don't know about that.... I'm no expert.'

Sashok held the certificate up to the light.

'It does have some sort of watermarks,' he said with less than total confidence.

In the meantime the carriage had gradually been filling up with passengers and Sashok had attracted some curious glances.

'It's total nonsense,' Sashok concluded.

'Don't be so sure,' said Harry as he rapidly stuffed the contents back into the briefcase. 'But I have to admit: the stakes are getting bigger.'

'You don't mean this certificate may be genuine, do you?'

'God knows ... but there's something about the whole set-up that I don't like.'

'You can say that again!'

'Gosh, I don't like it at all. Perhaps.... Will you object if I walk with you for a bit?

'Walk with me? What for? You promised ... about Nastya....'

'Yes, but the situation is changing. I now think that the main thing is for me to stay closer to you for a while. I'll arrange somewhere for you to spend the night in London. For the time being you can't go home. And then when I will be sure that you are safe, I'll deal with those clowns, too,' said Harry, adopting such an amusingly disdainful expression that Sashok nearly burst out laughing, despite the dramatic character of the situation.

Repressing his inappropriate laughter Sashok coughed and asked in as stern a voice as he could,

'And by the way, what did you manage to accomplish yesterday? Did you find nothing in the course a whole day?'

'Less than I wanted ... but enough to strengthen my suspicions.'

'What then,' said Sashok, lowering his voice, 'do you mean to say that ... they're really planning to ... do away with me?'

'That would be the logical conclusion, wouldn't it?'

'Well in that case, Anna-Maria is in danger, too!'

'Yes,' said Harry without looking at Sashok. 'It would be a good idea to ask her to stay away from home for the next few days.'

'I think she'll do that.'

'That's excellent. And it might be an idea to get her parents to go and stay with the aunt in Brighton. I know they promised to visit her ... but they need to be quick.'

'What? Are you trying to be funny? How do you think I am going to do that? Am I supposed to phone them and tell them that they've got to drop what they're doing and get themselves down to Brighton?'

'Mister Tutov, I have heard that at work you are given the most difficult problems which others can't deal with. They say that your thought processes may be a bit on a slow side but the results in the end are always brilliant. If they give you time to think a problem through then there's nobody like you. That's what they say of you. So come on, think of something!'

And with these words Harry made a show of turning away from Sashok so as to give him a chance to concentrate.

After a couple of minutes Sashok spoke again,

'Got it! I'll phone them and say that Anna-Maria and I are trying to patch things up. And I'll drop them a broad hint they would be helping us a lot if we could be alone together at home for two or three days. That should do the trick.'

'Well done!' exclaimed Harry, 'now I can see why everyone speaks so highly of you. Just one thing, though; when you phone them, don't say where you are. In fact, don't tell anyone…….you'll have to lie about it.'

'Do you think … do you seriously think someone might be listening in?'

'Everything is possible. If it's the KGB then it's easy for them, via a satellite.'

Harry suddenly stopped talking. Sashok was speechless too, after such a revelation. But then he suddenly remembered that today he had firmly resolved not to let panic take hold of him and so he tried to occupy his mind by studying the new French carriages. And he had to admit that he couldn't help admiring them. Instead of the disintegrating antediluvian bench seats full of the dust of ages with their dirty, sticky upholstery; instead of the stained and unwashed windows and the iron doors with their crude steam-age handles; instead of all this repulsiveness there was now a symphony of slender lines of bright metal, plastic and glass. Then there were the dark grey seats covered in a thick pile, displaying subtle designs, and tastefully tinted windows. Above his head was a glass shelf framed with grey and dark orange-coloured metal. And mounted in the shelf, moreover, there were individual reading lamps which could be turned on or off at the flick of a switch. The air-conditioning worked silently and unobtrusively marking an end to the draughts which were the curse of British trains. And how smoothly the new carriages moved along the rails! No worse than anything on the continent.

'Well, what do you think of it?' Sashok asked Harry, enthusiastically pointing things out with his arm.

'Oh, yes,' he answered, frowning, 'it's all a change for the worse. They've swapped our fine old trains for this French rubbish.'

'You don't mean you don't like it? The air conditioning works and it's not too hot, not too cold.'

'Yes, they're recycling stuffy air. What an unpleasant smell, don't you feel it? It was so much better on the old ones; the air was always fresh and everything was ventilated naturally. And everybody had his own door and window. And the steel lasted forever.....the trains travelled up and down and the doors banged endlessly and there was never any problem. But this lousy stuff will be falling apart every two weeks. These blooming doors will be the first to break down, you mark my words.'

Sashok shrugged his shoulders, realising that there were no arguments that could persuade the old bullhead. He tried to concentrate and remember why the name Ertera sounded vaguely familiar. He thought he might have heard about it briefly on the news, but he could not exactly put his finger on it. Harry was also silent, no doubt working out a plan of action.

Each engrossed in his own thoughts, they reached London Bridge. When they stepped down onto the platform Harry whispered, 'I'll walk a few paces behind you.'

Well, if that's the way it has to be. Sashok thought it was a stupid idea. As if this old, fat man could protect anyone from anything, let alone the KGB? Or from the world famous Russian mafia? What could he do against Dynkin and Lyosha? Sashok suddenly felt awfully tired of the absurd thriller he was living in. And a strange thought suddenly occurred to him: maybe all he had to do was to shake his head and this whole hallucination would disappear like a puff of smoke? And why on earth did he entrust himself to Harry? What if he were yet another character in this practical joke, in this endless palaver? 'So what you've got to do, then,' Sashok's inner voice suddenly piped up, 'is get on to Gavrilov in Moscow on his mobile phone. He's good at weighing up a situation at a distance.'

'It's expensive to phone a mobile, but then it's an exceptional case,' Sashok agreed, 'but how can I phone? I've no money on me and I've left my phone-card at home. Perhaps I could follow Vugar's example and quietly abuse my position in the office? I will wait till

Singh goes to the toilet or something.... But then how could I do it so that my colleagues wouldn't hear?'

Amazingly, both Sashok and his haughty inner voice had completely forgotten that in the office, at Century Building, fundamental changes had taken place over the past twenty four hours. But then to any normal person the events of the previous day would have seemed like a dream.... And a delirious one at that. So Sashok walked into the office wondering out of habit how to slip past Mister Singh without being noticed. And he was a bit baffled at first when he saw that his colleagues had all lined up to meet him and that first in line was Mr Singh. Harry, of course, came in after Sashok but the presence of a security guard only aroused even greater respect in the workforce. Mister Singh took Sashok to one side and said,

'Mister Tutov, I think it would be better if you took my cubicle now. We don't want you stuck out in the main office. And for the time being your bodyguard can sit at Liz's desk, and later on you and I might want to discuss how to re-arrange the layout. That is, of course, if you intend to spend much time with us'.

Sashok nodded graciously. The idea of ruling the roost from Mr Singh's booth amused him greatly. And the question of his phone call to Moscow was solved once and for all.

'Thank you,' he said, 'as it happens, I do have to make an urgent phone call to Russia. It's about a confidential matter.'

Gavrilov was categorical. As soon as Sashok told him how events were developing he burst out laughing,

'I don't know about the mafia, the KGB or drama students ... if you ask me that's all nonsense. But this Harry ... he's obviously the one you should be suspicious of. Haven't you guessed why he wants to get you all out of the house? You haven't? Well it's obvious! He wants to clear the place out. When he can be sure there'll be no-one at home.'

This sounded so logical that Sashok at once agreed.

'Yes, of course, you are absolutely right! I can't believe I didn't figure it out myself. I feel so ashamed! Anyway, that's definitely the end of my dealings with this buffoon!'

'Exactly! And my advice would be not to delay. Get rid of him right away. And warn your parents-in-law not to step outside their house for the next few days.'

When he had hung up the receiver Sashok surveyed Mr Singh's little work station and then waved imperiously to Harry as if to say 'Come here, my little friend.' And Harry immediately jumped up obediently and came running like a little dog. His face was beaming with joy and he was holding in his hands the copy of a pink newspaper: The Financial Times, the newspaper for the City and for investors and mandarins with high foreheads. It was opened at the pages devoted to financial data; the pages which Sashok never bothered to read but which he would occasionally glance at admiringly over the shoulders of a snooty passenger sitting next to him on the train. He was about to say something sharp and abusive but Harry displayed such joy and obviously sincere excitement as he ran towards Sashok that it completely changed his mood. In fact, Harry did not give him a chance to speak. Grabbing Sashok by the arm he said to him in a loud whisper: 'Do you know how Ertera PLC shares are doing today? My God, Mister Tutov, you're married to a multi-millionairess!'

CHAPTER TWENTY TWO

The world turns upside down

The blunt face of the Charing-Cross express had already appeared from the direction of the White Cliffs of Dover when Sashok spotted Harry. He was wearing his inconspicuous raincoat, with his cap pulled down over his eyes. 'Here he is, turning up as a bad penny' thought Sashok pretending not to notice him.

The train was only a couple of minutes late, but to Sashok's disappointment, it was made up of the rickety old museum piece carriages. 'Were yesterday's French coaches just some kind of reverie?' he thought. 'To be sure, everything that has happened recently seems like one long dream. Or, rather, nightmare.'

There was nothing for it but to get on the train. And in any case Sashok intended to follow at least one piece of Harry's advice, i.e. stick to his old routine and behave as though nothing had happened. It had to be 'business as usual.' This would protect his sanity, but it was easier said than done. True, it was not difficult to get out of bed, as usual, at 6.15, prepare and gobble up his porridge or pour milk onto a bowl of cornflakes. Nor was there any problem about dragging himself to the station, getting onto the same tiresome train, and reading The Times for the whole journey. But would he be able to keep his cool if his colleagues came out to meet him again or Mr Singh started looking searchingly into his eyes to seek approval for his managerial actions?

Yes, this was the climax of the whole practical joke: the purchase, in his name, of the small publishing company where he was employed, to put it mildly, in anything but a leading capacity. At first it seemed to Sashok that somebody was simply having a laugh at his expense. Then he came to realise that all those around him, including his boss, the truculent Mr Singh, although stunned, did take him seriously. He put up manful resistance when the client from Tiraspol dragged him and Mr Singh off for dinner at the Savoy. Sashok, obviously, had read that nowadays the Savoy is considered somewhat dated and that rich and famous go to Nobu or the Ivy, but for him a trip to the Savoy was like stepping into the forbidden world of exotic luxury. Sashok resisted as best he could, mumbling something about the pressure of work and other duties. 'Perhaps', he said, 'it might be better if you and Mr Singh go by yourselves.' But to no avail; the wretched Moldovan was determined to take the 'boss' along as well. 'But I'm not even the boss!' Sashok wanted to cry out, my colleagues are just having a laugh, but he didn't dare. In addition Mr Lupanu evidently exaggerated the historical significance of the publishing company and considered it some kind of a 'front' behind which some rather shady but clearly extremely lucrative deals were made. Mr Singh, damn him, played up to the Moldavian guest, assuming a very serious and meaningful expression. Then, when Mr Lupanu asked about Century Buildings' contacts with the City, the Indian even indulged in a little name-dropping, mentioning a few double-barrelled surnames which Sashok had never even heard of. In the end Sashok derived no pleasure from tasting the salmon in an improbable lobster sauce, nor from the 'Sancerre' rosé wine or from the servile waiters.

To be honest, what kind of a proprietor was Sashok? He couldn't take himself seriously in this role. And what was going to happen to him when the misunderstanding was sorted out? (And it certainly would be sorted out, probably sooner rather than later). What Sashok really wanted was just to return to his former, humble but clearly defined and predictable existence. His only ambition was once again to be editing articles on Moldovan textiles, Lithuanian energy supplies or about anything else. And even Mr Singh, in his heart of hearts, realised that Sashok was an editor sent from Heaven and that there was no comparison between him and Vugar and Tsveta and the Russian Korean Lee who all worked in that miserable pot-boiler of a publishing house which had been rapidly cobbled together with whatever came to hand in an effort to siphon off money from naïve Russian advertisers. Everyone knew that only Sashok and nobody else was capable of saving the stupidest and most hopeless article, that in a few hours he could turn a piece of uninformed idiocy into a peach even when everyone else had made a hash of things and were shrugging their shoulders in despair. Everybody understood that the miserable little establishment was no place for somebody like Sashok but that it was still early days and that once he had served his apprenticeship in the Tiraspol textile industry, etc. he would move on to new horizons. But for the time being (and it was shameful to admit it but it was a fact) the hackwork he was involved in brought him satisfaction. What a joy it was for him to string words together, weave them into patterns and create musical rhythm, tempo, melody and hypnotic phrases out of nothing.... 'You really are a maniac, a fanatic....that's what you are!' Anna-Maria would say. She would pretend she was disapproving of him. But Sashok was not easily taken in; he had made a sufficient study of these English ways to know that this was really a compliment, an expression of sincere admiration and perhaps even pride in a beloved, if somewhat eccentric, husband. After all, it has to be remembered that eccentricity here was quite respectable, even if this was rarely said aloud. On the other hand, ordinariness was acclaimed and held up as an example, but in reality it was often quietly despised.

It was an irrefutable fact that Sashok was a kind of human word processing machine, a compulsive editor-writer. Give him anything which required editing, rewriting, restructuring and Sashok was your man – and a happy one. The subject matter was almost immaterial to him: what difference did it make? An absurd idea took hold of him: what would happen if he made his way unnoticed to his office desk, humbly sat down and asked Mr Singh to give him something to edit? As if it was the most natural thing in the world. Would everything suddenly go back to being the way it was before? But deep in his heart he of course knew that he could not extricate himself from this hell so easily. And on top of everything else he now had to worry about some steel shares which somebody had bought in his wife's name.

Meanwhile, at home ... well, things were not good at home either. Anna-Maria had not spent a night at home for almost a week as she was annoyed at Sashok for some trivial nonsense. And his beautiful Russian lover Anastasia had lost all interest in him; she never called (although she promised she would) and was possibly even involved in some shady dealings…..at least if Harry was to be believed. But Sashok was not inclined to believe him now. Harry meanwhile walked past Sashok, nodded casually and muttered 'Hi-yah' as people do when they're greeting not-so-close acquaintances, especially when they can't remember those not-so-close acquaintances' names. Sashok felt offended and thought 'What's got into him?'

But Harry soon turned and walked back majestically and then flopped onto a seat opposite as if he were exhausted and said,

'So, then, you decided not to follow my advice and you spent the night at home.'

Sashok just shrugged his shoulders as if to say 'I'm a free man and this is a free country so I'll spend the night wherever I wish'. Then he said,

'And you, where did you spend the night?'

'Well, I had to protect a certain important person. Because this important person is behaving irresponsibly and carelessly.'

'Pack it in, Harry. You didn't spend the night under my bedroom window standing guard.'

'Oh yes, I did.'

'I find that hard to believe. You weren't hired as a bodyguard. You were hired as a detective. You'd be more useful in London gathering intelligence around the Cornwall Hotel.'

'And where do you suppose I was in the evening? I was right there. I don't mind telling you that these were tense hours. The work was hard and involved big risks.'

'So what did you discover?'

'Well, for example, *that man*, on closer inspection, was not really so like you after all. The rest was make-up, laid on pretty crudely by the way. Look a bit closer and you realize he's noticeably shorter than you and much older.'

At this point Sashok choked and all his steely determination to maintain an independent and cold manner with Harry seemed to evaporate.

'So why then did he look so convincing to both of us on the station?'

'Well, first there was the effect of your habitual clothing; it had been very carefully chosen. Second, he's obviously a high-class actor and, no two ways about it, he had learned to copy the way you walk, your gestures and even facial expressions!'

Sashok felt a real chill, and a shiver ran down his spine.

'You know, Harry, I've got to be honest with you…..The fact that somebody has spent a long time observing me, has learned how to copy me and is now going around impersonating me…..and that people are maybe looking at him and thinking it's me – for some reason all this makes me feel very strange.'

'Alexander, I would feel exactly the same in your shoes,' Harry answered, rummaging about in his raincoat pocket. 'But have a look at this piece of paper.'

'What's this?'

'It's a photocopy of the passport belonging to the woman you know as Anastasia.'

'Tsybakina. Alevtina Mikhailovna. Place of birth: the city of Omsk,' Sashok read, thunderstruck. 'Look,' he said, 'she's three and a half years younger than Anna-Maria…'

'Yes, and here's a copy of the passport page with her British visa. It's all in order; the visa was issued by the British Embassy in Moscow.'

'Wait a minute…. what about the grapes then?'

'What grapes? What do you mean, Alexander? What's this about grapes?'

'She didn't come here via the Channel Tunnel then?'

'Of course she didn't. Why should she make things difficult for herself? It's a normal tourist visa valid for six months....and there was an Aeroflot ticket for flight SU-241.'

'There was a ticket? Where?'

'In her handbag. Where else would it be?'

'Which means you've been in her handbag? That's theft! How could you?' shouted Sashok (but then he checked himself: it was a stupid point to make to a professional thief and burglar).

'Don't forget, Mister Tutov, that this lady is attempting to steal something far more valuable.... And by the way, I had to take an enormous risk – all for your sake, mind you! – and get into her room in the Cornwall Hotel.'

'You didn't! Did I ask you to do anything like that?'

'Believe me, there was no other way. Unfortunately, I had to make it look like theft.'

'But this is simply unbelievable! And was Nastya so fast asleep that she didn't hear you? Or did you ... stifle her?'

'What do you take me for? No, of course not. If you remember her room is in the basement and there's a little window.... And I managed to choose a moment when she was very, very busy.'

'Busy doing what?'

'Well, if you really want to know.... She locked herself in the bathroom ... with him.'

'Locked herself in? In the bathroom? With him?'

Sashok was about to ask: why? Not because he was that stupid, but simply because he really did not want to work out what it was so unpleasant to work out.

'Yes, they were so distracted that they were completely off their guard. They were making such a noise that they couldn't hear anything. Strange noises, indeed, as if someone was being thrashed with a belt or something like that. Then there was more shouting. It was so loud that I thought the people in the neighbouring rooms would come running in and spoil everything. She even left her bag on the table in the room. And the man, he left his jacket on the chair. So I quietly opened the door and....'

Sashok was sitting with his back to Harry and was biting his lips. A burning, dark sensation such as he had never experienced before rose up from somewhere deep down inside him. Finally he got a grip of himself and said almost cold-bloodedly,

'OK then. What happened next? What did you do with the passport?'

'I took a copy and ditched the original by Charing Cross police station.... And it only took a couple of minutes before a bobby picked it up.'

'What was the point of that?'

'The police were bound to take note of the fact that she had deviated from the tourist route specified in her visa. So now she has attracted their attention and I wouldn't be surprised if she's already on flight SU-242!'

'Well OK ... but what else did you find? Any money?'

'Yes, there was some money and I had to take it....otherwise who'd believe it was theft? And I also had to have a rummage about in his pockets, just to make things look right.'

'And did you come across any documents?' Sashok asked quickly.

'No. Only a credit card, a Visa Platinum. And there was quite a lot of cash.

'And whose name was the credit card in?'

'Here it is. Have a look: Nikolai Ostrov ... yes, Nikolai Ostrovsky.'

'Ah, yes, a famous Soviet writer. Ruined his health for the sake of Glorious Communism. Wrote a novel about his experience called 'How the Steel was Tempered.'

'What steel? You're rather confusing me today, Alexander. First you talk about grapes and now about steel or something. But......yes, yes, forgive me for being a bit slow on the uptake.... Of course! That explains everything! The green grapes and then steel, steel, steel! That's the answer to the problem. Mister Tutov, that's some powerful brain you've got there! I take my hat off to you!'

Struck by this outburst, Sashok could not bring himself to disappoint Harry on the question of his intellectual abilities. 'Maybe he is playing me along? Lord knows. His face looks quite serious, though, but I'll be damned if I understand what he's on about,' thought Sashok. Whatever it was, Sashok decided to deflect Harry from his enthusiasm for his intellectual might.

'So then, let's sum up,' said Sashok in a business-like manner, 'you took their money, you took the passport in the name of Ana ... I mean Ms Tsybakina.... You took Ostrovsky's credit card....'

'And then there's this,' said Harry, taking a small, elegant and evidently expensive mobile phone out of his bottomless raincoat pocket.

'What's it?' asked Sashok with a look of disgust on his face – he didn't want to be anywhere near this stolen object.

'Ms. Tsybakina's telephone,' Harry answered, sheepishly.

They spent the next fifteen minutes discussing the way that the latest models of mobile phones are configured. And how to extract the last twenty numbers from the memory.... Those which Ms Tsybakina had dialled or those which she had been called from.

'Look carefully. You may recognize some of them. I'll check the London numbers myself and you look at these foreign ones. Those beginning with 7 are for Russia, aren't they? Look how many there are.... 7095, 7812, 7916, 7903....'

'No, no,' said Sashok agitatedly as he ran his eyes over the numbers, 'I've never seen these before....This one is the code for Tiraspol..... Of course, I phone the town now and again but it's not this number. We'll have to check....'

And then.... Then Sashok suddenly felt as if he had been hit in the chest. Among the outgoing numbers he saw a Moscow one which was very familiar indeed. In fact it was one of the few which he knew by heart.

'No ... *nevozmozhno* ... it's impossible.... It simply can't be.... I must be dreaming,' he muttered under his breath in Russian.

'What's up?' Harry blurted out. 'What does that mean - *nevozmozhno*? What's not possible?'

But Sashok did not reply. He just clenched his teeth and straight away called the number with no thought for what would happen next.

'Alya,' an unmistakable velvet voice said in the ear-piece. 'How many times have I told you not to phone me on this number? You're supposed to be an intelligent woman but sometimes you behave like a complete idiot. Any communication has to be through Koryaviy, or in an emergency through the reserve switchboard.'

'Valyera,' Sashok said in a sombre tone, 'this is not Alya speaking. And it's not Nastya either. This is Alexander Tutov.'

The person at the other end suddenly hung up.

Sashok's world has turned upside down.

CHAPTER TWENTY THREE

The masks are off

'Who was that and what did they say? Come on, give me a translation,' Harry demanded.

But Sashok was sitting, stroking the phone as if he had taken leave of his senses. Then at last he said:

'I can't believe it, Harry. This kind of thing only happens in nightmares. That mobile number belongs to Valyeriy Gavrilov, my best school friend and that was his voice on the phone. And judging by what he said he is a close friend of Nastya's, or of this, whatever her name is, Tsybakina. He is apparently in secret communication with her.'

Harry wanted to say a few words of comfort, but....

Both of them shuddered in surprise, and Sashok almost dropped the phone, because, loudly and brazenly, right in his hand, it began to play the tune of a racy Russian folksong 'Karly-Marly, Old Grey Beard'. The whole carriage could hear it.

Sashok hesitated for a second, looked despairingly at Harry (he was nodding his head fiercely as if to say 'answer it, for God's sake!') and then at last he pressed the button with the green telephone receiver icon.

'It seems we got cut off,' said Gavrilov in a hoarse voice. 'It's actually a good thing you called, Sasha. I've been meaning to give you a ring, anyway.'

'Really? So you you've been meaning to give me a ring, haven't you?' Sashok interrupted angrily. 'And what's this 'good thing' you are talking about, eh? You ... how do you expect me to react after what you have done to me? I thought we were supposed to be friends!'

'You're right, you're right,' replied Gavrilov, 'but listen, we can turn it around. Alya's already on her way to the airport and the whole team's packing their things. So don't get mad. Don't get mad, OK?'

'What do you mean, don't get mad? Look, I rather like pranks myself but there are limits!'

Sashok vented it all on Gavrilov: the accumulated irritation of the last few weeks, the upset and anger, the sense of helplessness and even that dark feeling which had emerged from some shameful depths. He could not stop himself as he roared and yelled and thundered. Harry, meanwhile, waved his hands at him in vain, exhorting him to calm down as the whole carriage was getting agitated.

At last Sashok got tired and fell silent for a second allowing Gavrilov to chirp in.

'Stop shouting like that' he pleaded. 'Listen to me, Sasha. This business you've got.... What's it called? Century or something? Well, we'll leave it to you as a sort of compensation for all the inconvenience caused.... Of course it's not such a big deal, it's not the Bank of New York. But it could be turned into something useful. It's got lots of potential for brokerage of all kinds. I know an oil company in one of the autonomous regions which wants a listing on your stock exchange and I could perhaps put you in touch with each other. Do you know what IPO is – Initial Public Offering? No? Oh well, it doesn't matter.... You've got an Indian in that company of yours, who's no fool. You should take notice of what he says. He's got a good head on his shoulders. Look, you and I will do some more work together.'

'Work together? Are you taking a piss? No way! I'm not even sure that I have the slightest inclination to ever talk to you in the future!'

'You'll cool off, you will, believe me. Now, listen to what I have to say. Hold on to this blessed publishing business of yours. But the steel shares, you've got to give that back. Do you understand what I'm saying?'

'I don't care a damn. First the grapes, then the steel.'

'You will care all right when they slit your throat. And, believe me, they will, for that kind of money. You'll have to give it back, and quickly.'

'Oh, what kind of nonsense is this....'

'Oh, it's no nonsense! I don't know anything about the grapes, but the shares in Ertera Plc, you will have to give them back as a gift or sell them back for a token amount. Our accountants will be in touch with you soon.... Actually tomorrow. Or, perhaps, even tonight. So don't be stubborn and don't even think about procrastinating; just do exactly as they tell you. They're really the tops, these accountants, not like any you've ever seen before. So don't quibble. And tell your wife it's a matter of life or death, yours, mine, hers.... Quite literally.'

'Explain to my wife! Are you serious? Tell me how I'm supposed to go about doing that. How can I tell my wife what has happened when I don't understand it myself?'

'Well OK, OK! What don't you understand? This is neither the time nor the place to go into great detail but I might be able to give you a few pointers. So go on, ask me. If I can give you an answer, I will.'

Sashok almost choked with indignation but then suddenly realised that something else had awakened inside him, something which had successfully penetrated all the layers of his righteous anger. And this something, of course, was curiosity. 'What a strange creature is a man!' Sashok thought to himself, and then aloud, he said,

'Very well. Tell me, Gavrilov, does this guy Byenik work for you?'

'Oh, yes, he does. Who else would he be working for? He's a talented fellow, don't you think? He's a trained actor, a prize-winner by the way. He's a good improviser. But he's not without weaknesses, the blighter....'

'And what about his crazy name? What nationality is he?'

'He's Russian, of course.... Well, at least half-Russian. He liked the nursery rhyme that starts *Eniki-Byeniki-Vareniki* and so he acquired the nick-name 'Byenik'. He got so used to it that he always answers to it now. But his real name's Misha Grigoriev.'

'And is that Dynkin also one of yours?'

'Did you like him? He's a tough nut, isn't he?' Gavrilov laughed, but there was something unpleasant in his laughter; it was nothing like the way he used to laugh when they were at school. Then he seemed to switch the laughter machine off and press the serious conversation button. He said,

'No, things are far more complicated with Dynkin.... We're from different teams but we were brought together for this mission and first we were working together. But we had some disagreements along the way.... I suppose in England you are taught the importance of being a team player? Well with oafs like that in the team it all came undone. It was largely their fault that everything ended so badly.'

'I am not so sure about the bad ending. ' countered Sashok. 'Seen for my side the result is not all that awful. For example my wife and I are still alive. But tell me, why did those petty crooks of yours dump me with those shares?'

'Oh, yes, sorry about that. That was stupid. Everything went haywire. Believe it or not, those blithering idiots took you for Grigoriev.... Because as always they were drunk. Oh, if Russians didn't drink they'd have conquered the world ages ago.'

It seemed to Sashok that he had completely lost the thread.

'To hell with your Grigoriev and with Ertera. I'm more interested in where you found this girl.... Alya?'

'Aha!' said Gavrilov triumphantly, 'Now, isn't she really amazing? You couldn't tell them apart with your wife! The first time I saw her she took my breath away. Can you imagine it? It was on Rostov railway station and she looked like a flayed cat but I said right away that she was the double of an Englishwoman that I knew. We washed her down, gave her a lick of paint and dressed her up.... She came out pretty well, didn't she?'

'So, when you saw her you had a brainwave to put on this ... firework show?'

'Well, yes, something like that.'

'And set up a honey-trap for me? You spread some honey, fool rushes in and the trap is sprung.'

'No, Sasha, you've misunderstood. I....'

But Sashok suddenly felt overcome by unbearable sadness, he felt so awful that, unexpectedly even for himself, he pressed the red button on the handset. Then he switched off the phone altogether.

Harry looked at him in surprise. He maintained a respectful silence for a minute or two but then could restrain himself no longer and asked,

'Did you discuss the problem of the Ertera shares?'

'Yes, we did,' Sashok answered reluctantly. 'My friend insists that I hand them back.'

'Why? You should do a bit of bargaining.'

'Harry,' said Sashok, 'if I don't hand them back they will kill me.'

'According to the business plan they should have killed you already, but they didn't. There are defensive measures you can take.'

'I'm tired of your defensive measures! And now I remember where I heard about the damned Ertera. This morning I was shaving and listening to the radio, although I admit I wasn't paying much attention. They were talking about some Russian oligarch who wanted to get his hands on the company. It appears he was buying up shares through third parties. For some reason he wasn't allowed to buy them directly. So he was trying to get his own people on the board of directors. But then he ran out of luck. Something didn't work out. It was a stupid little mistake; they didn't submit a document on time or something. A power-of-attorney was not certified. Then someone missed a flight. And then late yesterday evening, or overnight, the opponents of this hostile bid were able to call an extraordinary meeting and buried the whole business. And that, my dear Harry, is why Anna-Maria and I are still alive and it's got nothing to do with your protective measures. It now looks as though the Serious Fraud Squad is getting involved…..'

Harry lowered his eyes, sniffed and eventually said,

'They're already involved,' Mr Tutov, 'and have been for quite a while.'

'What? Who's involved?' asked Sashok

'The Serious Fraud Squad. A department which investigates serious economic crimes'

'So you ... you were deceiving me as well!'

'Where's the deception, Alexander? Was it by helping you and probably saving your life?'

'But you … you're not….'

'Who aren't I, Mr Tutov? I assure you I really am a pensioner. But before I retired my life was … let's say, very colourful and varied. Believe me, fate is quite unpredictable, and it doesn't always depend on the individual…. I'll tell you in the strictest confidence, that in my young days I found myself frequently operating on both sides of the law. Do you understand what I mean? But then the day dawned when I recognised the sins of my youth and atoned for them. Sometimes of course the atonement was quite nicely rewarded. I was always considered a master of my craft … on both sides. And now you can see that I'm old and poor. I'm sure you know that pensions here … well, you know they don't go very far. But you can find work on the side, freelance.'

Sashok, in stunned silence did not know what to say.

Then Harry decided to take the initiative.

'Do you want to hear my theory? ' he said. 'I think they were undone by greed.'

'And booze,' Sashok added.

'Well, yes, that too. They came up with a good scheme and worked out the details. It is obvious your old school friend knew the various techniques. But either he didn't know them well enough or he hadn't had much practice, or maybe there was some other factor involved….I don't know. He's obviously talented but he's a bit of an amateur. If he had had a bit more staying power he could have got a bridgehead here and gone on to do lots of other things. He would have had a structure in place for laundering money, for company take-overs and lots more besides. By the way, Anna-Maria's father is a highly respected man in the City and his daughter's name alone could have opened a lot of doors. But at the last moment your compatriots turned out to be short of resilience and patience. And greed. They were undone by greed.'

'And drunkenness,' said Sashok.

'Probably drunkenness too. But the point is they were within striking distance of their goal when this steel magnate appeared. I imagine he had made an approach to his old KGB chums who are now leading businessmen, of course, and asked if they had anyone who could help him sort out a problem he had in London. They answered that there'd be somebody there soon. They said they were working on a mixed English-Russian couple whom they would either recruit or swap for some illegal agents. The guy they've already driven half out of his mind and they've planted a classy and well-trained female agent on him. This guy's as good as ours already, they said, he's hooked and it would soon be time for some serious work. But the oligarch told them that 'soon' wasn't good enough. He needed something right away, tomorrow, yesterday more like. He'd be ready to pay two, three or five times as much. Well, they went wild and decided to take a risk and shorten the deadlines. And it all fell apart.'

'But does that happen with professionals?' asked Sashok.

'Anything can happen! You haven't heard about the legendary uncatchable bank-robber who left his wallet behind one day with all his documents so he was sent down for 30 years? Then there was the famous Soviet intelligence officer, a master conspirator, who came unstuck when he left a micro film in the pocket of a jacket he'd taken to the dry-cleaners!'

'Probably been drinking too.'

'Possibly that too. But then even Homer sometimes nods.'

'In Russian we say: *I na starukhu byvayet prorukha* - even old wise woman can have a lapse.'

'More expressive in your language. But these aren't the olden days. Both in Russia and in Britain today, for every true professional you'll find two ex-policemen (or militiamen) and a bingeing bandit. That's why you have to bring in the pensioners.'

'And what about the grand old gentleman who drove me about in a limo and plied me with whisky? Is he a pensioner, too?'

'Definitely! He's an old acquaintance of mine. Where haven't we bumped into each other! Sometimes on the same side and sometimes on different sides. Now he's also on a pension and does a bit of work on top. But what a bunch of people to get mixed up with: Dynkin and the Uzbeks!'

'And that's what I don't understand. Where do the Uzbeks fit in?'

'Ah, yes. Your black friend Dynkin comes from Tashkent where he's been gently double-dealing with locals, drove them mad there. So he decided to sell you to them and even convinced them that you were the spitting image of a relative of the steel magnate's wife, a person the tycoon couldn't stand. True there are complicated clan relationships in play but that fool Dynkin didn't understand any of that. Oh! Human greed! And James, that friend of mine, has behaved disgracefully in his old age. I'm telling you: pensions here are very small so people get involved with any damn business.'

'It just seems improbable that a genuine aristocrat, a real patrician....'

'But that's it. He's been cashing in on it all his life. And people who weren't born with such good looks, who didn't go to a private school – they have to slog away all their lives, strain their brains to the point of burn-out. All comes back to the same thing: an indecent pension! So I hope you've made provision for yours. Alexander. If you haven't, you won't find it easy living on the basic state pension.'

'Well, I ... first of all I've got to buy a house and then....'

'No, no, you've got it wrong, believe me! I can suggest one or two interesting possibilities, 'Legal and General' 'The Prudential' 'Norwich Union' and a few others.'

'Ah you work on the side for them too!?'

'Well, who can blame me for that? For you I'll only take a minimal commission, I promise! And in addition, some of these companies offer excellent house insurance against fire, theft, burglary etc.'

'Now just hang on a bit, Harry. There is something I still don't understand. So please, put your sleuth's hat on again and explain something to me. Surely, nobody in his right mind could possibly take that girl ... Tsybakina ... for an Englishwoman?'

'Of course not! But, mind you, she wouldn't have gone onto the board personally. She'd have hired a local lawyer or a go-between, somebody like Mr Singh, and he would have voted in her name at the shareholders' meetings. There are all sorts of ways of doing it.'

Sashok was silent for quite a while, and then said,

'I'd like to think that Nastya, or whatever her name is, wouldn't have let those thugs see me off.'

Harry looked at Sashok with a mixture of suspicion and pity. Then he replied,

'I prefer your alcohol theory. Byenik got drunk out of his mind and got into a street-fight with the Yardies.'

'You mean the Jamaican gangsters?'

'Yes, I do. And now Byenik is hardly alive. He's badly cut up, covered in plaster and bandages and he's due to be emergency evacuated to Russia. Sounds about right?'

'Absolutely. But it's a bit boring. I can't help thinking that Nastya ... she can't be all that horrible. It's just this world that made her do those dreadful things. Maybe in fact there are parallel universes where she is somebody's nice wife.'

'Alexander, don't start getting all mystical! Otherwise I'll give you a lecture along the following lines: before you start distinguishing your world from another you've got to learn not to get confused about your briefcase, your wife and yourself! But come on, let's have a glass and then – home.'

'What is there for me to do at home?' Sashok said gloomily.

'Oh, you're wrong,' said Harry. 'This time you've got plenty to do at home. According to my information Anna-Maria is coming home today as well.'

'What!' exclaimed Sashok, 'and all the time you knew and never said a word!'

'Er ... yes, well, I didn't have the right to,' Harry replied, embarrassed.

'Now I get it!' said Sashok, feeling angry. 'You've kept her hidden away all this time.'

'Yes, but not from you, Alexander. She was in serious danger.'

'Still, how could you make such a fool of me?! Not very nice of you personally or of that bureau you work for. What's it called? The Remarkable Crimes Office? I was completely lost and so were her parents, to put it mildly. You've taken years off their lives.'

'Or saved them....'

After this tetchy exchange Sashok and Harry both went into a bit of a sulk. But then the platforms of London Bridge appeared through the window and Sashok, after a moment's hesitation, suddenly grabbed his briefcase and, hugging it to his chest, headed for the exit.

'Wait! Just a second!' yelled Harry. I didn't have time to tell you something important.'

'What else is there to say?'

'I didn't have time to tell you that Byenik's and Miss Tsybakina's passports are fakes. But the quality is unbelievable. Genuine works of art, an absolute delight just to look at!'

'So what's that to me?'

'Well, it probably means there are no such people as Grigoriev and Tsybakina.'

'I see. That means Gavrilov is still lying to me. Well, I don't give a damn. What's it got to do with me? It doesn't matter as I'm never going to see these people again....'

'If I were you I wouldn't be so quick to say that. Anything can happen. In fact, I have a feeling that you'll meet them again one day.'

'Rubbish.... Goodbye, Harry, time for me to go home now. Don't forget to send me your invoice.'

And so saying Sashok jumped off the train onto the platform. Opposite him he could see the white sides of the new French carriages of the train which was about to set off in the opposite direction.

Sashok burst into a run like a real sprinter and just managed to jump on board as the doors were closing. But Harry, running after him, was not so lucky. Now he was standing on the other side of the window and was trying to say something.

Sashok suddenly cheered up.

'Well, well, what is it that you are so eager to tell me, oh freelance detective of mine?' said Sashok, confident that Harry could not hear him. 'Get a hold of yourself: is that the way Englishmen behave? You've become a real Russian.'

Suddenly the doors opened again for a second. Harry thrust his head into the carriage and said in a loud whisper,

'Just one bit of advice! Believe an old man's words! Don't mention Miss Tsybakina to Anna-Maria.... Wise men don't tell.'

Then the doors closed for the last time and the train moved off bearing a brooding Sashok eastwards. And a rather sad and pensive Harry stood all alone on the platform.

ACKNOWLEDGEMENTS

I would like to thank David Morton for helping to edit the text and suggesting numerous improvements. Many thanks also to Elena Priestley for her amusing artwork (see the cover), and to Gabriel Gatehouse for his contribution to the translation. Above all, thanks to Alex Tulloch, without whom this novel wouldn't have existed in English. The novel was first published in Russian by the Vremya publishing house, Moscow, in 2006.